Praise for David Sowell's
The Masters: A Hole-by-Hole History of America's Golf Classic

"It is often said that the real Masters doesn't begin until the back nine on Sunday. Mr. Sowell's nuanced descriptions of those holes make it clear why the chase on Sunday afternoons is so often thrilling."

—John Paul Newport, *Wall Street Journal*

"Every kind of book on the Masters that could be written had been written, until David Sowell came along. He takes a route previously not taken, giving each of the eighteen holes of Augusta National its own fifteen minutes of fame."

—Furman Bisher, the late legendary sports columnist for the *Atlanta Journal-Constitution* who covered the Masters for more than sixty years

"Sowell gives us the Masters in full flower."

—*Booklist*

"An entertaining read that enthusiasts will enjoy."

—*Library Journal*

"A rich historical view of the course where success breeds legends and where failure can haunt even the most brilliant golfer's career. . . . If you are a golf fan or enjoy watching this tournament that is the unofficial start of spring, *The Masters* is one of the best books on the sport and this tradition."

—Jason Schott, *Brooklyn Digest*

"We have always wondered why the Masters is a tradition unlike any other. David Sowell has an answer. . . . He covers the magical moments of the good, the grand, and the also-ran on a course that itself is a memorial to Bobby Jones."

—Sidney L. Matthew, author and producer of *Life and Times of Bobby Jones*

America Tees Off

AMERICA TEES OFF

True Tales of Golf's Rich History

DAVID SOWELL

University of Nebraska Press
LINCOLN

Manufactured in the United States of America

The University of Nebraska Press is part of a land-grant institution with campuses and programs on the past, present, and future homelands of the Pawnee, Ponca, Otoe-Missouria, Omaha, Dakota, Lakota, Kaw, Cheyenne, and Arapaho Peoples, as well as those of the relocated Ho-Chunk, Sac and Fox, and Iowa Peoples.

For customers in the EU with safety/
GPSR concerns, contact:
gpsr@mare-nostrum.co.uk
Mare Nostrum Group BV
Mauritskade 21D
1091 GC Amsterdam
The Netherlands

Library of Congress Control Number: 2025010735

Designed and set in Fanwood Text by K. Andresen.

Dedicated to the memory of my father,

Frank H. Sowell, a true member of the Greatest Generation

Contents

Acknowledgments

I could not have done this without the tremendous support of my family: my wife, Susan, whose love is more appreciated than she will ever know; sons Brett and Brandon, who have always been ready with support and advice when needed.

Thanks to my agent, Robert Wilson of Wilson Media, and to Rob Taylor and his team at the University of Nebraska Press.

And last but not least, the friends and golf partners whose support along the way has been much appreciated: Dr. Cordell Scott, Art Gill, John DeBlasis, Gale Tieder, and Ethan Edwards.

America Tees Off

THE FATHER OF AMERICAN GOLF

In the fall of 1887, Robert Lockhart, a Scottish transplant who resided in New York City and who was in the fine linen trade, made a trip to his hometown of Dunfermline, Scotland, to purchase linen goods. During his trip Mr. Lockhart took a break from his business responsibilities and made the forty-mile train trip to St. Andrews, which was then, as it is today, the undisputed world capital of golf. His destination was Old Tom Morris's Golf Shop at the St. Andrews Links.

No one has ever left a greater imprint on golf than Old Tom Morris. He was Jack Nicklaus, the legendary club maker Karsten Solheim, a magnificent golf course designer à la Donald Ross, and a superb golf instructor like Butch Harmon all wrapped up in one. His crowning achievement as an instructor was his son Young Tom Morris. Young Tom was beating his father on the course by the age of thirteen and had matched his father's total of four British Open titles by the time he was twenty-two. Sadly, Young Tom passed away at the age of twenty-four from a pulmonary hemorrhage.

Old Tom's shop was just a few paces off the eighteenth green at the St. Andrews Links. He had opened it in 1866, and by this time he employed eight craftsmen, who were turning out clubs and balls bearing his name. The shop was filling orders from around the globe, but none were from the United States. But that would soon be changing, thanks to Robert Lockhart.

It is not known what time of day Lockhart entered the shop. If it was after Old Tom's daily morning round, Lockhart may have encountered the shop's famous proprietor. Old Tom loved to talk golf with the shop's customers. With the smell of gutta boiling on the stove for that day's ball production permeating the establishment, he would stand among the shavings that covered the floor, explaining to a would-be buyer the qualities of the various components that were used in club making—dogwood, persimmon, apple, hickory, and ash.

Often Old Tom would take a customer to a special place in the shop. The special place was Young Tom's locker filled with his clubs and club-making tools. As the customer would gaze at the locker's contents, Old Tom would say, "Undisturbed since he last touched it."

When Lockhart departed the shop that day and made his way back to the train station with his purchase of six golf clubs and two dozen balls neatly packed in a box, the residents of St. Andrews who saw him would have surmised there was nothing special about it. However, this was indeed a very special purchase, as it would trigger a golf explosion in the United States.

Along with another fellow Scotsman, John Reid, and several others, the group broke in the clubs and balls in a cow pasture in Yonkers, New York. More clubs and balls were ordered. The group soon moved to a thirty-acre field just down the road and laid out a six-hole course.

In November 1888 the group formally formed a golf club. They chose to name the club after the world capital of golf, St Andrews. And they vowed to hold themselves to the same high standards that were observed there. To distinguish the club from its namesake back in Scotland, an apostrophe was added; their club's name would be St. Andrew's Golf Club. Some years later the *New York Times* would acclaim Robert Lockhart as the "Father of American Golf."

THE MOST FLAMBOYANT PLAYER ON TOUR OUTDOES HIMSELF

Doug Sanders was a rags-to-riches story. He grew up dirt-poor in rural Georgia and was a self-taught golfer. He won the Canadian Open as an amateur in 1955, and he won his first event as a professional two years later, the prestigious Western Open.

Sanders was famous for his attention-grabbing, flamboyant attire, earning him the nickname "Peacock of the Fairways." But Sanders's clothes never grabbed as much attention as his arrival by ambulance did for his second-round tee time at the Pensacola Open in early March 1962.

Sanders, who had won five times on tour in 1961, had departed the course the day before in a tie for third place, after firing a five-under-par 67. In his motel room that evening, he stepped on a piece of glass from a broken ashtray and cut a small gash in his foot. He didn't think it was serious and dressed the wound himself.

The next day when he arrived at the Pensacola Country Club to warm up, he began to have intense pain from the wound, and he was hurriedly taken to the emergency room of a nearby hospital. There a physician examined his wound and found it contained a shard of glass.

The doctor removed the glass, redressed the wound, gave him medication for the pain, and released him. Since there were only a few minutes left before Doug's scheduled tee time, he was rushed back to the course by way of an ambulance, with its siren screaming.

The ambulance delivered Doug to within just a few yards of the first tee with just mere moments to spare. Grimacing in pain, Sanders limped onto the tee. Amazingly, he birdied the first hole, thanks to an approach shot that left him two feet from the pin. He hung on for pars on the next two holes, and then the pain medicine kicked in. With much of the pain subsiding, he played the next fifteen holes at four under for his second straight 67, giving him the lead by three strokes.

Much improved, Doug shot another 67 on day 3 to keep his three-stroke lead. He slipped slightly in round 4, falling into a tie at the sixteenth hole, but a birdie at seventeen won him the tournament by a stroke.

YOUNG TIGER OVERCOMES A ROUGH PATCH

In 1997 Tiger Woods overcame plenty of adversity to win his first professional tournament outside the United States, coasting to a ten-stroke victory in the Asian Honda Classic in Bangkok, Thailand.

It was not an easy week for Tiger; he had to fight off the effects of jet lag, a stomach virus, lost luggage, and comments by his mother to the press about his marital future. The win was Tiger's fourth victory in just twelve starts as a professional. He shot a steady two-under-par 70 in the first round and then took command of the event with an eight-under-par 64 in round 2, followed by rounds of 66 and 68. In his third round, he thrilled the gallery when he drove the green at the 389-yard tenth hole.

First place paid $48,000, which was icing on the cake for Tiger, as he reportedly received $480,000 as an appearance fee. Not bad for a trip whose primary mission was to please his mother, Kultida Woods, a native of Thailand. She had met Tiger's father, Earl, twenty-six years earlier when he was in the United States Army and stationed in Bangkok.

Mrs. Woods arrived in her homeland with much fanfare two weeks ahead of Tiger. While appearing on a popular Thailand TV talk show, it was reported in the media that she had told viewers that she would demand that Tiger marry a Thai woman. When she greeted Tiger at the airport, he immediately questioned her about what she had reportedly told the TV audience. She said: "I never said that. The dadgum media got it wrong. All I said was that it would be nice if he did." Two days later Tiger told journalists, "I will marry whomever I fall in love with."

A YOUNG EXECUTIVE GOES ROGUE

In 1892 Spalding, the sporting goods company, sent young Julian W. Curtiss to England to examine its leather industry as a possible source of supply for footballs. While there, Curtiss ventured out onto a course, and the golf bug nailed him. He decided on his own that there could be a buck to be made in the United States with golf, and he purchased a small inventory of golf equipment to sell back in the States.

When Curtiss returned to corporate headquarters, his golf purchases became the butt of jokes around the office. His coworkers dubbed his golf inventory purchase as "Curtiss's Folly." A. G. Spalding, the company's founder and chief executive officer, was resolved to write off the purchase as a learning experience for his young executive.

Undaunted, Curtiss talked two of his neighbors into the construction of a five-hole course across their combined acreage. Soon other neighbors wanted to try the game, and the modest amount of golf inventory he had purchased began to move and then was totally wiped out when members of Shinnecock Hills Country Club, Tuxedo Country Club, and St. Andrew's in Yonkers became aware that the Spalding Company had golf equipment.

Reorders were made, and golf soon developed into a major product line for the company. By the spring of 1894, Spalding was manufacturing its own line of clubs. A year later, A. G. Spalding had a nine-hole course built on his estate. In 1898 the company began producing golf balls at its Chicopee, Massachusetts, facility. In time golf would make up 40 percent of the sales for the company, and Julian Curtiss would become its president and serve in that capacity for several decades.

BABE RUTH AGREES TO BECOME A YANKEE AT THE EIGHTEENTH GREEN

In early January 1920, the biggest deal to date in professional sports took place: the sale of Babe Ruth by the Boston Red Sox to the New York Yankees for $125,000. Before the Yankees would sign off on the transaction, they wanted their manager, Miller Huggins, to locate Ruth and make sure he was on board with the deal. It meant Huggins would have to travel by train from New York to Los Angeles, where Ruth was enjoying the closing days of December 1919.

Shortly after his arrival, Huggins learned that Babe could be found at the public golf course at Griffith Park. He waited patiently for Ruth to complete his round. After Ruth putted out on the eighteenth, the two huddled just off the green. Huggins reviewed the terms of the deal with Babe and what Babe's compensation would be from the Yankees. Babe gave his blessing to the deal.

Two months later, scores of Yankee fans were at Penn Station to get their first glimpse of Ruth as he and the Yankees departed for spring training in Florida. It would be a scene that would be repeated many times over the years: Ruth boarding a train with his golf bag slung over his shoulder.

That first year with the Yankees, the club trained in Jacksonville. Unseasonably cold weather greeted the team on their scheduled first official day of practice and Ruth's first appearance on the field in a Yankee uniform. Because of the cold temperatures, management made that day's practice optional. All but a few headed for the diamond. Ruth was among the few. He headed to the golf course.

Babe became the first athlete on the American scene whose popularity swept from the sports page to the general public at large. With fifteen daily newspapers in the New York City market and it also being the base of operations for several wire services and news syndicates, Ruth was constantly in the news, not only during baseball season but in the offseason as well. Besides baseball, the other near constant in stories about him was his golf.

In the early 1920s, interest in golf in certain parts of the country was quite strong. But across the nation, the game was far from being mainstream. The son of a saloonkeeper, Ruth's domination of America's pastime made him the ultimate hero of the common man. As a result of the large amount of press coverage Babe's golf was receiving, a tremendous amount of interest in the game developed among his ever-increasing legion of fans, and they were heading for the course in droves.

The Yankees' front office wasn't too fond of Ruth's preoccupation with golf. Their top executive, Ed Barrow, would seethe with rage when Babe dashed from a spring training workout to the golf course. But he chose not to make an issue out of it. If golf was a threat to a player's performance, Ruth had to be immune to it.

Ruth's golf was instrumental in sending other major leaguers onto the course, and this was foreseen as a problem by many in the baseball hierarchy. Until the original Yankee Stadium, aptly called "The House That Ruth Built," opened in 1923, the Yankees shared the Polo Grounds in Manhattan with the New York Giants for their home games. Before Babe joined the Yankees, the Giants, managed by the legendary John McGraw, were the big boys on the block when it came to baseball in New York City. McGraw managed the Giants from 1904 to 1933, guiding them to ten National League pennants and three World Series titles. McGraw stood only 5 feet 7 inches tall and was aptly nicknamed "Little Napoleon."

He was arrogant, abrasive, and tyrannical. Beginning in 1921, McGraw managed the Giants to four consecutive National League pennants and two of his World Series titles. Before the start of the last season of this four-year run, McGraw became concerned that the increasing popularity of golf among his players would hurt their performance on the field. So, on the first day of spring training, McGraw barred his players from playing golf until the season was over.

Another baseball legend joined McGraw on the anti-golf side of the ledger: Ty Cobb. He played a good bit of golf but had not been able to get his game out of the '90s. When he became the manager of the Detroit Tigers, his golf playing all but ceased. He went one step farther than McGraw. He confiscated his players' golf clubs. Cobb, one of the top hitters the game has ever known, was convinced the long, carefully timed stroke used in golf wreaked havoc on a baseball player's performance at the plate, where a shorter and quicker stroke was required.

Another well-known figure in baseball at that time made headlines when he joined Cobb in trumpeting the belief that the golf stroke was detrimental to a baseball player's hitting: Umpire Bill Klem. One of two umpires selected for baseball's Hall of Fame, Klem had garnered the nickname "the father of baseball umpires." During this period umpiring crews did not rotate assignments, and the crew chief worked home plate. As a longtime crew chief, Klem had logged over two thousand games behind the plate. With that amount of tenure at the back of the batter's box, his opinion on a hitter's swing carried sizable weight in the baseball community.

Klem's opposition waned, however, and in a couple of years, he had taken up golf and would join Ruth on the course in Florida during spring training.

ARNOLD PALMER RESUSCITATES THE BRITISH OPEN

After Ben Hogan's win at the British Open in 1953, interest by Americans in playing in the event began to wane significantly. Playing the British Open had always been a challenge for American players. It involved a lengthy and expensive journey. And given the paltry prize money, you might not break even if you won the tournament. In 1959 only three Americans were in the field.

The fuse that would trigger the British Open to again become a target for American players and restore much-needed prestige was lit in 1960 in Denver, Colorado, at the first tee of the Cherry Hills Country Club.

Cherry Hills was the site of the 1960 United States Open, and its final day produced one of the most exciting finishes in its history. Over a half-dozen players, including Ben Hogan and a twenty-year-old amateur named Jack Nicklaus, had a shot at the title. When it was over, Arnold Palmer, the winner of the 1960 Masters, who had started the final round seven strokes behind the leader, was the winner.

Palmer started that final round by unleashing a massive drive that reached the green of the par-four 346-yard opening hole. He two-putted for birdie and then birdied five of the next six holes. When the day was over, he had shot a 65 and won by two strokes. Jack Nicklaus was the second-place finisher.

In 1953 Ben Hogan won the Masters, the United States Open, and the British Open. The day after his win at Cherry Hills, Arnold Palmer announced he was going to the British Open at St. Andrews in three weeks in an attempt to match Hogan's 1953 feat.

Despite being the winner of two majors that year, Palmer had to play his way into the field in a thirty-six-hole qualifier. He did so with ease.

Three other Americans qualified, one of whom was the winner of the event in 1932, fifty-eight-year-old Gene Sarazen. He bettered Arnold by one stroke in the qualifying. In 1922, shortly after winning the United States Open, Sarazen lost his job as the head pro at Highland Country Club in Pittsburgh over his desire for extended time off to compete in that year's British Open.

Arnold was in the top four on the leaderboard after each of the first three rounds. On the last day, Arnold started four strokes behind Australian Kel Nagle; he made one of his patented charges but came up one stroke short.

The big winner was the British Open, and the excitement and interest that Arnold's participation had generated boosted the standing it needed as a major championship. This surge in interest continued to skyrocket when Arnold won the event in 1961 at Royal Birkdale and in 1962 at Troon.

GOLF GRABS MICHAEL JORDAN

In March 1984 Michael Jordan was alone in his dorm room at the University of North Carolina. He was at a low point. Days earlier, he and his Tar Heels had lost to Bobby Knight's Indiana Hoosiers in the semifinals of the Eastern Regionals. Michael's performance in that game had not been up to his usual standards. He had just 13 points before fouling out.

Michael's alone time ended when his teammate and roommate, Buzz Peterson, and a friend of his showed up. Peterson's friend was a member of UNC's golf team and a future PGA Tour standout. His name was Davis Love III.

Buzz informed Michael that he and Davis were heading over to Finley Golf Club in Chapel Hill to hit some balls. Michael asked if he could tag along. Once there Michael was bitten by the golf bug, and he would become one of the country's utmost devotees to the game.

Michael's zeal for the game was more than reflected by the golf marathons he enjoyed. One of these marathons occurred in May 1997 at Miami's Turnberry Resort & Spa, Michael teed it up very early in the morning with the goal of playing fifty-four holes. He didn't quite make it. Darkness fell and ended his effort at forty-eight holes.

Michael played again the next day in Miami, not on the golf course but on the basketball court. He and his Chicago Bulls teammates were going for a sweep of the Miami Heat in game 4 of their semifinal playoff series. Michael's performance, at least for almost three quarters of the game, was dreadful. He made only two of his first twenty-one shots from the floor. The first one did not go through the net until well into the third quarter. But in the fourth quarter, he was pure Jordan, scoring 18 consecutive points in one stretch and cutting what had been a 20-point deficit to just 1 with two minutes to go. The Heat hung on, however, and pulled out an 87–80 win.

Michael's forty-eight holes the day before had been the talk of press row before the game. When quizzed about it in a postgame interview, Michael, who finished the day as the game's leading scorer, with 29 points, said: "I don't think that had anything to do with the way I played today. I'm not going to blame what I did today on what I did yesterday."

Michael and the Bulls would win the series in the next game and then defeat the Utah Jazz in the NBA Championship Series four games to two.

PRESIDENT OBAMA CUTS HIS GOLF SHORT FOR GOOD REASON

President Barack Obama played golf over three hundred times during his presidency. One notable round in May 2011 had to be ended early. He played just nine holes on that day at the course at Joint Base Andrews Naval Air Facility.

The members of the White House press pool who accompanied him did not think anything was amiss. Maybe it was just due to the cool and rainy weather that day. Little did they suspect that in just a few hours they would be reporting on the biggest story of Obama's presidency.

He was headed for a top-secret meeting to review final preparations for a military operation he'd approved two days earlier, the one involving a raid by Navy SEALS in Pakistan that would end with the death of Osama bin Laden.

In retrospect they should have realized something was up when he made a beeline to the West Wing instead of going to the residence quarters of the White House. The last forty-eight hours, however, had not produced any indications that something huge was unfolding. President Obama had given no hint of it as he went about his duties consoling tornado victims, delivering a college commencement address, and cracking jokes at a black-tie dinner.

That Sunday evening, Obama, still in his golf attire, Vice President Biden, and Secretary of State Hillary Clinton, along with other key personnel, were waiting for events to unfold in the White House's Situation Room. They dined on sandwiches brought in from Costco. When the operation commenced, they watched it unfold on a live feed from the scene.

At 11:35 p.m. President Obama went on the airwaves and announced the operation, and that bin Laden had been eliminated.

GOLF INFECTS THE UNITED STATES' TWO RICHEST MEN

As golf began to take off in America in the early 1890s, it was perceived by the country's rank and file as an activity of the rich. This perception was more than solidified because of the country's two richest citizens, John D. Rockefeller and Andrew Carnegie. The two men took up the game in the early 1890s, and they would approach golf with the same passion they exhibited in building their vast empires, Rockefeller in oil and Carnegie in steel. Rockefeller's entry into golf required a well-organized covert action, while Carnegie openly came to the game through association with other native Scotsmen.

The demands of amassing one of the world's largest financial empires had taken its toll on Rockefeller. When he was in his late fifties, he experienced a lengthy period of poor health. His doctor ordered him to spend less time on business and more on recreation and relaxation. The seeds of his golf addiction were planted during a game of horseshoes, when his opponent remarked that his long, smooth pitching motion had the makings of a first-class golf swing.

Rockefeller chose to act on his friend's suggestion. But first, there was a competition problem that would have to be overcome. The competitor was Rockefeller's wife, Cettie. She had already taken up golf. There was no way John D. was going to be outplayed on the course by his spouse. Covert actions had often played a part in John D.'s business dealings, his venture into golf would also begin with one.

The operation took place at The Country Club in Glenville, Ohio, which was just a short carriage ride from the Rockefeller estate in Cleveland. The goal of the operation was to practice in secret, until such a time that Rockefeller's golf skills surpassed those of his wife. The club's pro, Joe Mitchell, was his instructor and headed up the operation. It involved seven caddies. Four were involved in shagging balls, and one was charged with teeing up balls for Rockefeller as he banged them out into the range in a machinelike fashion. The other two caddies were deployed as lookouts in case Mrs. Rockefeller showed up at the club. And one day she did. When one of the lookouts spotted her and shouted out, Rockefeller scurried into a cluster of nearby bushes.

The operation continued for several weeks before Mitchell declared his student ready for the big test. A few days later Rockefeller told his wife he was going to the course with her to give the game a try. Mrs. Rockefeller was stunned. She was even more stunned an hour or so later on the first tee at the club when her husband split the fairway with a solid opening drive. As his ball rolled to a stop, she exclaimed: "John, I might have known it. You do things better and more easily than anyone else."

Up until putting a club in his hand, Andrew Carnegie's chief exercise for the previous three decades was a daily two-mile walk around Central Park. He could have joined any of the New York area's most prestigious country clubs, but he chose to play his golf at St. Andrew's Golf Club in Yonkers, New York. Spearheaded by Robert Lockhart and his friend John Reid, some months after Lockhart's club purchase at Old Tom Morris's Golf Shop, the St. Andrew's Golf Club in Yonkers had formed and became the kickoff point for the golf craze in the United States. Carnegie shared a special bond with Lockhart and Reid. They, like Carnegie, had been born in Dunfermline, Scotland.

St. Andrew's Golf Club membership received an enormous benefit from Carnegie's allegiance. Since the club's inception, it had moved several times as a nine-hole course. When the membership sought to take St. Andrew's to the next level, Carnegie loaned the club the funds to purchase 160 acres in Westchester County and build an eighteen-hole course and a first-class clubhouse.

To ensure he was never too far from a fairway, John D. Rockefeller had courses built at his estate in Cleveland and his estate just outside New York City. He also bought a golf course in New Jersey, where he built a mansion that he named "Golf House." During the winter months, Rockefeller would head south, and his stays at Augusta, Georgia, helped establish it as a winter golfing haven.

Rockefeller was also one of the first golfers to have his swing photographed in various stages and from numerous angles, and he would spend countless hours poring over the stills. At one point he developed a problem with overactive feet during his swing. To cure this, he practiced with croquet wickets hammered tightly over his shoes until the flaw was fixed. When he had a period when he struggled to keep his head down during his swing, Rockefeller employed an extra caddie whose sole duty was to utter that reminder just before he pulled the trigger.

Rockefeller's legendary frugality was apparent when he played. Even as the oil baron's empire was reportedly making him three thousand dollars per minute, he would spend ten minutes searching for a lost twenty-five-cent golf ball. But there were other times when his golf urges would trump his thrift—like the time he mobilized a small army to clear snow from his Cleveland estate course so he could get in a round. Also, thrift never came into play with Rockefeller's attire. He was a staunch believer in the appropriate dress for any activity. So, when he was on the course, he was always decked out in tailor-made golf jackets and knickers and dazzling argyle sox.

Rockefeller developed alopecia in the 1890s, losing all of his body hair. After his hair loss, Rockefeller took to wearing a hairpiece. He had several pieces for ordinary wear, but he had two special ones made by a wigmaker in Washington DC. It took the man six weeks to fashion each hair covering, as each was formed hair by hair. One of these pieces was for Rockefeller to wear to church; the other was for golf.

Andrew Carnegie played as often as he could—even in the dead of winter, when his butler would bundle his 5-foot-3-inch frame from head to toe for the hour-long drive out to the course in an open car. The commute from his mansion in the city quickly became tiresome, so Carnegie built a well-appointed cottage a short distance from the clubhouse for overnight stays.

When Theodore Havemeyer, the first president of the United States Golf Association, died unexpectedly in April 1897, the *New York Times* reported that Andrew Carnegie's name was being bandied about as a possible successor.

A BIG OPENING IN TINSELTOWN

The biggest movie opening of 1924 was *The Thief of Bagdad* starring Douglas Fairbanks. It was the story of a lowly thief questing for the love of a beautiful princess. It featured flying carpets, winged horses, fearsome beasts, and an invisibility cloak. It easily finished the year as the movie industry's top-grossing film.

But for a large number of the Hollywood set both in front of and behind the camera, the biggest opening of the year in 1924 was not *The Thief of Bagdad*. The biggest opening of the year occurred four miles from the intersection of Hollywood and Vine, when Lakeside Golf Club opened its gates. Golf was booming in California, and nowhere in the state was the game hotter than with the Hollywood set. Lakeside was situated between North Hollywood and Burbank, which practically made it a next-door neighbor to all the major studios. Once Lakeside was open, it was no time at all before its membership roll was bursting with Hollywood stars, directors, and top studio executives.

In August 1929 the star-bursting membership at Lakeside became starstruck themselves when golfing great Bobby Jones paid them a visit. At this point in his career, Jones had won nine major golf championships and had reached the same super-icon status that Babe Ruth had achieved in baseball. He had claimed his third United States Open two months earlier and was on his way to compete in the U.S. Amateur at Pebble Beach. In 1929 the U.S. Amateur carried the same amount of prestige as the United States Open, and Jones had won the event four times out of the last five years.

When he arrived in California shortly before the Amateur, Jones received an invitation to play a round at Lakeside. When word reached the movie lots that Jones was on Lakeside, executives, stars, and crew slipped away and headed to the course. By the time Jones started the back nine, hundreds of spectators were lining the fairway. To Jones it was a practice round before a tournament, but for a day it resulted in movie production being slowed in Hollywood.

ANCHORS AWEIGH, SAM SNEAD

In April 1942, almost five months after the attack on Pearl Harbor, Sam Snead, who the week before had played in an exhibition with Gene Sarazen at the Naval Academy's new golf course at Annapolis, strode into a naval recruiting station in the nation's capital and enlisted.

Given a report date in mid-June, Sam had the opportunity to participate in one more major championship before beginning his World War II naval service, the PGA Championship. It was held at the Seaview Country Club in Atlantic City, New Jersey, during the last week of May.

At that time the PGA Championship was a match play event, preceded by a medal qualifying round to determine the thirty-one players who would join the defending champion, who was exempt from qualifying, in the thirty-two-man field. Sam struggled in the thirty-sixth-hole qualifier and was in danger of not making the top thirty-one until he played his last ten holes at four under par.

Sam carried the momentum from the late stages of the qualifier into his matches and made the finals. Sam's opponent in the final was Jim Turnesa, who was already serving in the army. He was playing thanks to a furlough he had arranged with his commanding officer at nearby Fort Dix.

Turnesa had a much tougher route to the finals than Snead. He had to defeat Ben Hogan in the quarterfinals and Byron Nelson in the semifinals. The match with Nelson required thirty-seven holes.

In the thirty-sixth-hole final, the gallery was all in for the underdog Turnesa. He fed off their enthusiasm, and at the end of the first eighteen, he was three up. He held that lead until the twenty-fourth hole when Sam turned it on. By the thirtieth hole, Sam was two up. Turnesa cut his lead to one. But at the thirty-fifth hole, Sam closed him out in dramatic fashion, chipping in from sixty feet for a birdie to go two up with one to play.

The win was Sam's twenty-eighth as a professional and was the first of his seven major wins. His first-place purse was $2,000, part of it in war bonds. Turnesa received $750. But he would not get to retain his winnings. As part of his arrangement with his commanding officer for his active-duty furlough, his earnings from the event were to be donated to the Army Relief Fund.

A PICTURE-PERFECT TACKLE

Streaking is the act of running naked or almost naked through a public area for publicity, as a prank, a dare, or a form of protest. It took off in the 1970s, with streakers doing their thing on televised events such as award shows, sporting events, and other large public gatherings.

Golf was not immune. Jim Furyk got to experience it twice. The first time took place during his 2003 U.S. Open victory. A very good-looking and buxom young lady who was topless tried to make her way toward him. Security was quick to intervene, and she came up a little short. At the 2010 Ryder Cup at Celtic Manor in Newport, Wales, at the eighteenth green in Furyk's Sunday singles match against Luke Donald, a man wandered out of the gallery. He was scantily clad. He wore a sun hat, red cape, socks and shoes, and a novelty G-string displaying a cartoon monkey over his crotch. He, too, was quickly dealt with by the security staff.

At the British Open at Royal Troon in 1997, young Tiger Woods had an encounter with a woman who was very fond of him. She was almost naked. She wore only underwear, while the rest of her body was painted to look like a tiger.

The most famous streaking incident in golf occurred in the final round of the 1985 British Open at Royal St. George's. It took place on the eighteenth hole as the pairing of Tom Kite and Peter Jacobsen were just reaching the green.

A man emerged from the gallery naked and ran around the green multiple times with security personnel in hot pursuit. As the chase went on, Jacobsen decided if the streaker got close to him, he was going to take him down. The streaker did, and Jacobsen stepped into his path and tackled him, and then security swarmed over the man.

Fluff Cowan, Jacobsen's caddie, who was standing a few feet away, described the takedown. "It was a picture-perfect tackle. The shoulder right in the midsection. . . . He got his head out of the way. Thank goodness!"

Jacobsen contends that the tackle cost him. His putt for par was affected by the indentations left on the green by the streaker's butt when he was brought down. The bogey caused Jacobsen to drop from a tie for tenth to a tie for eleventh.

A year earlier, at the FedEx St. Jude Classic in Memphis, Jacobsen had experienced another occasion that was not as extreme as his British Open incident. His playing partner, Gary McCord, bent down to line up a putt, and his pants split open. Normally, this wouldn't be a problem, but McCord was not wearing any underwear. Jacobsen came to his rescue but at a price. He reached into his bag and loaned him his rain pants for a "fee" of twenty dollars.

BRYSON DOES HIS THING

In 2020 the 120th edition of the United States Open took place at the Winged Foot Golf Club, located in Mamaroneck, New York, a northeastern suburb of New York City. Pushed back until September because of the COVID-19 pandemic, no spectators were allowed. The only individuals present other than the players and their caddies were the media, tournament staff, and Winged Foot members.

Winged Foot features two eighteen-hole courses, the East and the West. The West course has long been considered one of the top venues for competitive golf. In 2020 it was hosting its sixth U.S. Open. At 7,477 yards and par seventy, it features narrow fairways, deep rough, and sloped greens that have a long history of inflicting punishment. Its trademark is a brutal finishing stretch of five extra-long par fours.

Tiger Woods had certainly seen his share of tough golf courses. The last time the Open was at Winged Foot in 2006, he had missed the cut, marking the first time in his professional career that he had not played the weekend in a major championship. In the run-up to the 2020 Open, he didn't hesitate when asked where Winged Foot Golf Club ranked: "Well,

I think it's right up there next to Oakmont, and I think Carnoustie . . . I think those three golf courses, they can host major championships without ever doing anything to them."

Gary Woodland, winner of the 2019 U.S. Open at Pebble Beach, California, was also asked for his thoughts on Winged Foot's West course. "There are no tricks to it," he said. "You've just got to step up and hit good shots. The key this week is you've got to drive the ball in the fairway. If you don't do that, you're going to be wedging out, and you're going to be trying to hit wedges [third shots] close because you're not going to be able to advance it too far out of the rough."

No one could argue with Woods's assessment, but when it came to Woodland's comments, they would be proved wrong by the winner of the event, Bryson DeChambeau.

The long-standing Open formula of finding the fairway went out the window when DeChambeau stuck a tee in the ground at the start of the first round. Leading up to the U.S. Open, DeChambeau's scientific mind; his set of clubs, all the same length; the way he went all out on every hole; his bulked-up body; and his ability to drive the ball farther off the tee than anyone who had ever played the game had the golfing world buzzing.

But before the Open, many believed that Winged Foot would take Bryson down. Among them was Rory McIlroy. He said this shortly after Bryson's winning twenty-three-under-par performance at that year's Rocket Mortgage Classic at the Detroit Country Club: "Wait until he gets to a proper golf course, and Winged Foot is as proper as they come."

But those predicting Bryson would be reined in at the Open were proven wrong. His style of carrying every bunker, of cutting every dogleg, of taking power over precision, had him in second one stroke behind leader Patrick Reed after the second round. After the third round, he was still in second, two shots behind leader Matthew Wolff.

In the final round Bryson blew by Wolff early on the front nine and played his best round of the tournament, a three-under-par 67. Wolff finished second, six strokes behind Bryson. Despite hitting only 23 of 56 fairways, Bryson finished the tournament at –6. He was the only player in the field who finished under par.

AMERICAN GOLF GOES PUBLIC

On July 6, 1895, the New York City Parks Department opened America's first public golf course at Van Cortlandt Park in the North Bronx. "Vannie," as it would become known, cost $624.80 to construct. Its nine holes were an unusual layout, as none of the first eight holes measured longer than 200 yards, while the ninth hole stretched out for over 700 yards.

Playing at Vannie was the polar opposite of country club golf. Chaos ruled. There was no charge to tee it up, and there were plenty of average citizens, both men and women, who were curious and wanted to try their hand at the recent craze of the rich and powerful. The chaos began when golfers exited the train at the nearby Van Cortlandt station and began their short trek to the course. They had to work their way through a mob of young street urchins desiring to be retained as caddies and constantly chattering, "Hey mister, have a caddie?" "Shall I carry yer clubs for yer missus?" "Caddie, sir, caddie, caddie?" Having a caddie at Vannie was seen as a status statement that the golfer could just as easily join a country club if only he wanted to.

Although few of the women retained caddies, they let their dress reflect that they, too, were country club–worthy by wearing the latest fashion.

Fine hats, silk hose, and high heels were quite the norm.

Once at the entrance to the course, the golfers grabbed a numbered ticket from the attendant. Then they headed for the first tee, where they would wait, sometimes for hours, among the throng of players for their number to be called.

How well the Vannie golfers were equipped varied greatly. A few had a full set of clubs, while most of the rest varied between a modest number to just two or three. Some were innovative, using twisted pieces of gas pipes as clubs.

Each day scores of individuals who had never swung a club before teed off. What they knew about golf etiquette they discerned from observing other Vannie players who also knew nothing about golf etiquette. Some would jump on the first tee and hit their tee shot, even though the previous group had advanced only fifty yards down the fairway. To make matters worse, the groundskeepers at Vannie also knew nothing about golf and often scarred the greens with deep ruts by pushing heavily laden carts across them.

If a golfer could survive teeing off at the first hole among the stares and the commotion of the throng behind him, the frustratingly long wait between shots, not getting struck by the shot of an impatient golfer in the group behind him, and made it to the tee of the ninth hole, he faced quite a test. This hole was three and a half times the distance of any of the previous eight holes, and an extra ball or two may be needed because of the two brooks that crossed the fairway and a different breed of street urchins. These urchins had found stealing golf balls produced a steadier and more significant stream of income than caddying, and with a lot less effort. They would position themselves in the woods and foliage that lined the long fairway and then streak out and make off with a golfer's shot, often before the ball even stopped rolling.

A SURPRISING DEFEAT LEADS TO A STELLAR COLLABORATION

In 1929 the United States Amateur Championship was held at the Pebble Beach Golf Links on California's Monterey Peninsula. Having won the event four of the last five times it was held, it was almost a foregone conclusion that Bobby Jones would take the event. When playing his second practice round at Pebble Beach, Jones solidified those expectations, setting a new course record with a five-under-par 67.

But in the first round of the Amateur, it was like an earthquake had rocked the Monterey Peninsula. The mighty Jones fell to a nineteen-year-old former caddie from Omaha, Nebraska, Johnny Goodman, in a match that was not decided until the final hole. In the gallery of almost two thousand that had followed the contest, there was almost as much gloom over the unexpected downfall Jones had suffered as there was an enthusiastic appreciation for the astonishing feat of young Goodman.

Jones's defeat would set the stage for the design of the Augusta National course four years later. The day after his defeat at the hands of Goodman, Jones was allowed to do something that he would not have had the time to do had he advanced in the Amateur. He traveled a few miles down the road and played one of the most talked about courses in the country—Cypress Point.

Jones found the course more than lived up to the buzz he had heard about it. He was enormously impressed with the way the architect, Dr. Alister MacKenzie, had laid out the course. Subsequently, the two had the opportunity to meet and found their ideas and thoughts on golf course design were finely in tune. When it came time to pick an architect for Augusta National, Jones chose MacKenzie.

MacKenzie's route to becoming one of golf's foremost course architects was a unique one. Initially, he was in the medical profession as a surgeon. He took up golf in his early twenties. In 1900, when he was in his late twenties, MacKenzie worked as a civilian surgeon for the British Army during the second Boer War in South Africa waged between British and Dutch settlers. The Dutch in South Africa were known as the Boers. They were vastly outnumbered by the British, so the Boer commanders decided to adopt the guerrilla style of warfare. The British eventually prevailed in the conflict.

MacKenzie had been intrigued by the effectiveness of the camouflage techniques the Boers had used. Soon after his return to Great Britain, he began to dabble in golf course design and incorporated a great deal of camouflaging techniques into his designs. When Britain entered World War I, MacKenzie served in the British Army—not as a surgeon but as an artillery officer. In this capacity he continued to study the art of camouflage.

After World War I, MacKenzie left medicine at the age of forty-nine to pursue a second career as a full-time golf course architect. Fourteen years later, when he arrived in Georgia to begin work on Augusta National Golf Club, he had designed over forty courses on four continents. The most noted among them, besides Cypress Point, were the West Course at Royal Melbourne in Australia; Pasatiempo Golf Club in Santa Cruz, California; and the Old Course at Lahinch Golf Club in Ireland.

When Jones and MacKenzie finished their collaboration in Augusta, they had constructed what many called the most subtle golf course in the country. Augusta National featured wide fairways and no real rough to speak of. By the standards of the day, it had very few bunkers. The greens seemed to be welcoming one's approach shot with open arms.

In keeping with MacKenzie's keenness for camouflage, the greens were an ambush. One slight slipup, and the player could find himself in a very bad way. If he was long, he could face a treacherous downhill chip or long putt. If he was short, he encountered tricky little mounds that seemed to vary in their dastardliness from one hole to the other. Most players were accustomed to encountering this type of situation at a few holes during a round, but the task at Augusta was withstanding it for all eighteen.

Throughout the years after Augusta National was opened, when Jones was complimented on the course, he would always be quick to point out that MacKenzie was the architect and that he had been his advisor and consultant.

IT WAS ALICE'S IDEA

On March 18, 1982, the Tournament Players Championship (TPC) at Sawgrass Stadium Course's seventeenth hole made its tournament debut and instantly became one of the most talked about holes in the game of golf. The center of the island green is only 137 yards from the tee, but the suspense it creates belies the hole's distance. After he has struck his tee shot, the player watches anxiously, hoping his ball is going to stay dry.

The legendary golf course architect Pete Dye created the course out of a swampy wilderness in Ponte Vedra Beach, Florida, and it was quite a challenge. He said this about how the hole came into being: "By the time we got to the seventeenth, we'd run out of things to think of." It was Dye's wife, Alice, who came up with the idea of an island green after she paid a visit to the construction site one day. Pete was not overjoyed with the idea, but he soon came around.

In addition to the carry over water, the green's location is in an area on the property that has a history of producing very windy conditions. In the gusty opening round in 2007, fifty tee shots found the water.

In that first TPC at the course in 1982, David Thore, from Reidsville, North Carolina, and a former collegiate teammate of Curtis Strange and Jay Haas at Wake Forest was in the first group off the back nine in that opening round, and he became the first player in the tournament's history to put his tee shot in the water at the seventeenth.

IT WAS DO OR DIE

Nothing in American golf quite rivals the emotion and tension of the Ryder Cup and the Solheim Cup. The player is part of a team representing their country. And if you are the visiting team, add in the rowdy opposing fans and you've got a recipe for ultra-pressure-packed golf.

Julie Inkster had proven she could handle the pressure of the LPGA Tour. She had racked up thirty-one victories that included seven majors, and six of those thirty-one wins had come in playoffs. But in 2015, while serving as captain of the United States Solheim Cup team, she knelt by the eighteenth green at the Golf Club St. Leon Rot, Germany. Unable to watch, Inkster was on one knee with her head down beside the eighteenth green, listening for the crowd to let her know what happened.

It was the final day of the singles matches. The U.S. team was in a big hole, having started the day trailing 10–6. The European squad, winner of the last two Solheim Cups, needed just four points out of the twelve matches that composed the singles competition to retain the Cup.

The scene that had Inkster placing her head down at the par-four eighteenth was the match placing the United States's Gerina Piller against

Caroline Masson. At this point six matches had already been decided, and the Europeans had reached a total of 13.5 points. A half in the Piller-Masson match, and they would retain the Cup.

Piller had a one-up lead at this point, but she missed the green with her approach shot, and her ball now rested in thick rough. Masson had struck a solid approach and was looking at a realistic birdie opportunity.

Piller's background was far from that of her fellow Solheim Cup teammates. She and her two brothers had been raised by a single mom. She grew up playing baseball and basketball with her brothers and was a member of a championship volleyball team. She did not take up golf until she was fifteen.

Family finances did not allow Gerina much exposure to the junior golf circuit. When she was a senior in high school, she played in a high-profile tournament that included Michelle Wie and Inbee Park. She had never experienced anything like that event. When she arrived at the driving range, her place was marked with her name on a placard. She said she hyperventilated. This was a world she had never seen.

Gerina played collegiately at the University of Texas at El Paso and had an outstanding career. She then toiled on the LPGA's minor league tour for three years before making it to the big time.

Ironically, what she found so appealing about golf was the individual challenge. In the team sports she had played before golf, she could play great and if the rest of her team struggled, they wouldn't win. Or she could have a bad game and her teammates could carry her. Golf was different. If she posted a good score, it was on her. If she struggled, she was completely exposed. Gerina relished that pressure. Now on the eighteenth hole in the Solheim Cup, she was facing the ultimate challenges in both the individual and team aspects.

Her chip shot from the heavy rough left her with a nine-foot putt to save par. While Masson studied her ten-foot putt for birdie, Gerina looked at the scoreboard and saw Europe stood at 13.5 points. If Masson made her birdie putt, she would give Europe the 0.5 point they needed to retain the cup.

Masson's birdie putt did not drop, but her par was good enough to win it for Europe if Gerina missed. She told herself: "This is do or die. This is what you practice for. This is like a once-in-a-lifetime deal here." She lined up her nine-foot putt, and as she did, team captain Inkster looked down at the ground. A few seconds later the roar from the crowd sent Inkster leaping into the air. Gerina had done it, winning a crucial point.

Five matches remained on the course, and the United States won them all to take the cup 14.5–13.5. It was the biggest comeback ever in the Solheim Cup's twenty-five-year history.

THE SELLER THOUGHT THE BUYER HAD MORE MONEY THAN COMMON SENSE

In 1895 the principals of a lumber company in the Sandhills of North Carolina were more than a little amused by their encounter with a man in his sixties from Boston.

Soon after the lumber company had finished a big project, extracting turpentine from the pine trees on a 10,000–acre tract and then cutting them down for lumber, the old gentleman from Boston showed up and expressed interest in buying that tract of land.

One of the principals with the lumber company was Walter Hines Page, and he wrote to a friend in New York describing what transpired:

> *I have had an amusing experience. There is an old chap from up in Boston who I fear has more money than good common sense. As he has this wild scheme in the back of his head that he can make a resort in these barren sand wastes . . . there* [are] *about 10,000 acres in all. I asked him to make an offer and he suggested that it might be worth one dollar an acre, but I closed the deal for 75 cents an acre. He gave me his check for $500 to bind the bargain, but I fear I will never see him again once he gets home and thinks it over.*

The gentleman from Boston did deliver on the remaining balance he owed and on his idea to build a resort. He was James W. Tufts, who almost five decades earlier, at the age of sixteen, had taken a job as a drug store apprentice. Tufts had gone on from there to invent a soda fountain machine that would produce vast riches for him.

Six months after the deal closed, the first phases of Tuft's resort opened. During development it was called "Tuftstown," and by its opening, it had been given the name Pinehurst. This name was chosen from a list of losing names in a contest to name a development in Tufts's home state of Massachusetts on Martha's Vineyard.

Tufts would soon make golf the cornerstone of his resort, with noted architect Donald Ross arriving in 1900 and designing four of the resort's courses.

GOLF LESSONS IN AN OFFICE SUITE IN THE HEART OF NEW YORK CITY

From the early 1930s until the late 1940s, Ernest Jones arrived to conduct his business Monday through Friday in Midtown New York City. His dress fit the location. He wore fashionable suits, usually blue, and, when they were available, a boutonniere from the garden of his Glen Head, Long Island, home.

The space from which Ernest operated was on the seventh floor of a Fifth Avenue skyscraper, two doors from Forty-Third Street, in an area given over to chrome and glass bank buildings, high-priced stores, and fervent shoppers.

The space Ernest occupied fell way short when compared to the others in the building. It was dusty and disheveled and lacking in sunlight. It looked like an abandoned pool hall. The two things Ernest needed to conduct his business stood out: a sizable rubber mat on the floor and a large canvas backdrop located twenty feet from the mat. Ernest, a very scholarly-looking man, was a golf instructor and thought to be the busiest golf instructor in the country. It is estimated that on average he gave three thousand lessons a year.

This demand for his tutelage was driven by the success of his pupils, who had won on some of golf's biggest stages. Those pupils included Virginia Wie, winner of the U.S. Women's Amateur three times; Gena Collet-Vare, winner of that event six times; and Lawson Little, winner of the British Amateur twice, the U.S. Amateur twice, and the British Open.

Ernest was born near Manchester, England. He began playing golf as a young boy, and by the age of eighteen, he was working as a golf professional. During World War I he joined the British Army. While serving in France, he fell victim to a German grenade and suffered the loss of his right leg just below the knee.

Ernest feared his golf career was over. After a four-month recuperation period, he was able to walk using crutches. He was soon fitted with a prosthetic and proceeded to attempt his first round of golf and shot an 83. A few days later he played again and shot a 72.

Ernest was soon working again as a club professional, and he immigrated to the United States in 1923. He developed and refined his theories on the golf swing and its instruction. He believed that everything taught by all other pros was bunkum. In taking your first lesson from Jones, you were requested to forget everything you had ever heard about the game. It is generally conceded that to hit the ball, you must keep your eye on it. Jones believed you could hit it with your eyes shut. He disputed all the usually accepted tenets of golf. If you asked him what was wrong with your swing, Ernest would say: "There's nothing wrong with any golf swing. The trouble is you don't swing." Ernest believed the key to hitting a successful golf shot was not the correct movement of certain body parts. Instead, the real key was the successful movement of the golf club.

Ernest instructed his students to take their normal stance and, utilizing only their hands, to swing the clubhead back and forth, gradually increasing the arc. This allowed the student to begin to feel the centrifugal force of the clubhead. His favorite mantra was "Swing the clubhead with your hands, and let your body be a follower."

As a student would be swinging a club, Ernest would play Viennese waltzes on a portable phonograph. He would often substitute other items for a golf club—a length of rope, a ball of wrapping paper tied to a string, and his favorite, a penknife tied to a handkerchief.

GOLF, BITTER COLD, AND PANTYHOSE

In early March 1980, Dave Eichelberger was wearing quite the ensemble when he stepped onto the tee for the last day of the Bay Hill Classic in Orlando. To counter the unusually bitter cold and extremely windy conditions he was facing, Eichelberger had on a white ski cap, a windbreaker, four sweaters, a golf shirt, rain pants, golf trousers, and a pair of blue pantyhose—extra-large. His garb and experience with cantankerous wind gusts in his native Texas proved to be the right combination, as he won the event by three strokes.

The tournament's first two rounds had taken place in ideal conditions, and Eichelberger had moved to the top of the leaderboard with a 66 on day 2. A brutal cold front with vicious winds swept in on day 3. The wind's speed reached forty miles per hour, and play had to be suspended.

Eichelberger and twenty-eight other players had to return to the course at first light the next day to complete their third rounds. The temperature with the wind chill factored in was in the mid-teens. That afternoon, when Eichelberger teed off for his fourth round, the temperature had climbed to fifty degrees, but the intense winds made it feel like it was in the thirties.

One of the early starting twosomes in the final round were Dave Hill and the tournament's host, Arnold Palmer. When they reached the tee at Bay Hill's very formidable par-three seventeenth, they were both nearly spent from the grueling conditions. Hill reached into his bag, pulled out a flask containing an adult beverage, and took a good swig. He passed it to Arnold, who took a good swig as well. Hill finished the round with a score of 80. Arnie shot 85.

Eichelberger finished the seventy-two holes at five under par to win by three strokes. The win was the high point of his career.

SCOTTIE RECORDS HIS FIRST PROFESSIONAL WIN

In May 2019 Scottie Scheffler picked up his first professional win. It came at the Evans Scholar Invitational on the Web.com Tour (now Korn Ferry Tour) at the Glen Club outside Chicago.

In the final round, Scottie fired a bogey-free, nine-under sixty-three—playing the back nine in thirty—to force a playoff with fifty-four-hole leader Marcelo Rozo. He claimed the win with a birdie on the second extra hole.

The twenty-two-year-old Texan had played collegiately at the University of Texas from 2014 to 2018. He was named "Phil Mickelson Freshman of the Year" and helped the Longhorns team win three Big 12 championships.

Scheffler, who began the day six shots off the lead, started strong with three birdies in his first five holes, then went on a tear after the turn, with birdies at 10, 11, 13, 14, 15, and 17. Scheffler had entered the week ranked No. 3 on the tour's money list thanks to six top-ten finishes, including a pair of seconds. His winner's check was for $99,000.

In addressing the media after the win, Scheffler said: "To get the first professional win is awesome, and it kind of gets the monkey off my back.

Hopefully, it'll lead to some bigger things to come." As of this writing, he has since won seventeen times on the PGA Tour, including four majors.

Since joining the PGA Tour in 2020, Scottie's career earnings total $60 million. Ironically, the benefactor of the tournament that was his first win as a professional, the Evans Scholars Foundation, was created by a golfer who had balked at accepting earnings he made in the game—Chick Evans.

Chick was one of the most acclaimed American amateur golfers of his time. In 1916 he won the U.S. Amateur and the U.S. Open to become the first golfer ever to do so. Bobby Jones would be the only other golfer to match that accomplishment. Chick was first exposed to the game as a caddie at the age of eight, at the Edgewater Golf Club in Chicago.

Chick spent his entire career as an amateur, winning twenty-two tournaments. To maintain his amateur status, he used the earnings from a golf instruction recording and a golf instruction book as the catalyst to create the Evans Scholars Foundation. Its purpose was to provide scholarship funds for caddies. Others in the golf community joined in to support the effort. It continues today as the largest scholarship organization in sports and the largest privately funded scholarship program in the United States.

Chick made his first appearance in the U.S. Amateur in 1909. He would play in the event every year it was held except one through 1962. In that first appearance, his bag contained just eight clubs. In his final appearance in 1962, his bag still contained just eight clubs.

USGA'S FIRST TOURNAMENTS AND USA GOLF'S FIRST CINDERELLA STORY

In early October 1895 the first U.S. Amateur and U.S. Open championships took place at the Newport Country Club in Newport, Rhode Island, played under the game's newly formed governing body, the United States Golf Association.

There were thirty-four entries in the amateur event, which was match play. The nation's first golf club, the St. Andrew's Club in Yonkers, New York, led the way in entries with nine. Each match would be eighteen holes, except the final match. It would be decided over thirty-six holes.

Much to the dismay of the large contingent of St. Andrew's members and supporters in attendance, their L. B. Stoddart, one of the pre-tournament favorites, was upset in the second round. But it would turn out that the St. Andrew's followers would still have much to cheer about—at least until the final match. Charles E. Sands, an outstanding lawn tennis player but an unheralded golfer, was considered the weakest of the nine St. Andrew's members in the field, but he became the tournament's Cinderella story.

Sands, who had only been playing golf for three months, claimed his first-round match without swinging a club, when his opponent failed to show up. He won his second match, four up, and his third, three up to reach the semifinals. The remaining semifinalists were Dr. Charles Claxton from the Philadelphia Golf Club, F. J. Amory from the Country Club in Brookline, Massachusetts, and Charles B. Macdonald out of the Chicago Golf Club.

Charles B. Macdonald grew up in Chicago. In 1872, at the age of sixteen, he was sent by his father to Scotland to study at St. Andrews University. While at St. Andrews, Macdonald took up golf with a passion. He was tutored in the game by Old Tom Morris himself and was granted the privilege of having a locker in Old Tom's shop. Macdonald soon became proficient enough that he played in matches on the St. Andrews Links against some of the best golfers in the area.

When Macdonald returned to Chicago, he became a stockbroker and made a passionate effort to establish a golf club in his spare time. But he could not generate enough interest and finally gave up the attempt in despair.

When the golf explosion started at the St. Andrew's Golf Club in Yonkers and reached Chicago, Macdonald took the point in the Windy City again. In 1892 he laid out a nine-hole course there in Wheaton and named it the Chicago Golf Club. A year later he added nine more holes, making the Chicago Golf Club the first eighteen-hole course in the United States.

Macdonald had breezed through his first three rounds with eight up, seven up, and four up wins. He faced off against Dr. Claxton in the semifinals and won handily, four up. The other semifinal between Sands and Amory drew most of the gallery. Sands's Cinderella story continued as he slammed the door on Amory at the sixteenth hole, when he went three up with two to play.

Those hoping for an exciting thirty-six-hole final the next day were sadly disappointed, as Sands's Cinderella story turned into a nightmare. Macdonald cruised to a five-up lead during the morning eighteen. And then he crushed Sands in the afternoon session by winning the first seven holes, to go twelve up with eleven holes to play and claim the championship.

The first United States Open was held the next day. Ten professionals and a lone amateur took part in its first edition, a thirty-six-hole one-day stroke play event. The lone amateur in the field, Alex Smith, was also the lone golfer in the field who had been born in North America—in Toronto, where he still resided. Of the other ten professional entries, seven had relocated from Scotland, and three were transplants from England. Horace Rawlins, the nineteen-year-old assistant pro at the Newport Country Club, who had arrived in the United States from England in January 1895, won the event by two strokes.

In the fall of 1887, Meadow Brook Club on Long Island missed a chance to be the lead in starting golf rolling in the United States. The club was considering adding golf to its list of activities. Two-time British Amateur champion Horace Hutchinson came to the club to demonstrate the game to the club's membership. After Hutchinson's demonstration, the membership elected to pass.

After St. Andrew's in Yonkers got the golf craze started, Meadow Brook joined the frenzy, opening a nine-hole course in 1894. Two weeks after the first Amateur and Open Championships, Meadow Brook played host to a challenge match that drew more attention than either of the USGA inaugural championships.

The circumstances that led to this match were spawned as a result of the U.S. Amateur at Newport. Charles Sands's showing in that event garnered the three-month veteran of golf plenty of attention. This irked many of those who were more experienced in the game, among them Winthrop Rutherfurd, who had lost to Charles B. Macdonald in the quarterfinals of the Amateur.

The ultra-wealthy Rutherfurd was a member of New York City's most elite social class and a direct descendant of Peter Stuyvesant, the last Dutch director general of New Amsterdam before it became New York.

Rutherfurd made disparaging remarks about Sands's golfing ability. When Sands was made aware of the remarks, he took offense. One thing led to another, and soon a match between the two for a $1,000 wager was scheduled at the Meadow Brook Club. The thirty-six-hole match took place on a Saturday two weeks after the Amateur Championship at Newport. It drew a large and very colorful gallery of New York City's upper class, with most men in colorful golfing jackets and the ladies in fine silks and stylish capes.

Sands, now a golfer for almost four months, carried the day, closing out the match at the thirty-fourth hole, when he went three up with two to play.

Rutherfurd lost not only on the course but in the clubhouse as well. During the match two men posing as guests of members gained access to the locker room and stole items from many lockers. Rutherfurd was the hardest hit, losing a gold watch and chain, the $1,000 in cash he had brought to pay off in the event he lost, gold cuff links, and two rings. The estimated total of his loss was in the $5,000 range. In today's dollars that would be about $100,000.

THE WINNING EIGHTEEN-HOLE SCORE WAS 132

On a cool November day, two weeks after the Sands-Rutherfurd match, the Meadow Brook Club on Long Island hosted another event, the first USGA Women's Amateur Championship. It was a one-day eighteen-hole affair, arranged on short notice.

Thirteen competitors would play in the event. Three competitors were members of the nearby Shinnecock Hills Golf Club, five were from the Morris County Golf Club in Morristown, New Jersey, three were from the Essex Country Club outside Boston, one was from the Newport Golf Club, and one was from Meadow Brook.

The Meadow Brook course was considered a tough track for men, and it would prove to be an extreme test for the women in the field, who had to tackle the course dressed in ground-sweeping skirts; using men's clubs, as no women's clubs were on the market yet; and playing from the men's tees, as ladies' tees were not yet in existence.

The favorites in the field were Martha Tenure, the ladies' champion from Shinnecock; another member of that club, Lucy Brown; and the ladies' champion of the Morris County Club, Howland Ford.

Ford's round quickly unraveled when she took a sixteen on the par-three third hole and then followed that up with three nines, a twelve, and a ten, to shoot 80 on the first nine. Mrs. Tenure came unraveled at the eighth hole, when she took a fifteen and finished her first nine with a 75.

Lucy Brown started with an eleven on the first hole and then played steadily, compared to the rest of the field, posting a couple of fours and a five to go with a few eights and nines. She finished her first nine holes with a 69. This placed her in the lead by one stroke over Miss N. C. Sargent from the Essex Club.

On the second nine, Mrs. Brown scored the only three of the day by the field at the par-three eleventh hole and seemed to have the event well in hand until she reached the sixteenth hole, where she took a twelve. On the seventeenth hole, she took a thirteen. At the last hole, a par four, she reached the green in five blows and then rolled in a thirty-footer for a double bogey to hang on and win with an eighteen-hole score of 132. Miss Sargent was the second finisher, two strokes back, at 134.

THE FIRST ROAR AT THE MASTERS

The roars that sweep across the Augusta National Golf Club during the Masters are one of the event's trademarks. They signal something big has occurred. For instance, Billy Joe Patton's hole-in-one at the sixth hole set off one of the greatest Sundays in Masters history in 1954. Arnold Palmer's legion of followers, known as "Arnie's Army," roared to let everyone on the course know their hero was making a charge in 1960 and 1962.

Perhaps the two loudest of the trademark Augusta roars came just minutes apart in the final round in 1986. When Jack Nicklaus, on his way to a phenomenal 30 on the back nine on Sunday and his sixth green jacket, dropped his second shot approach on the par fifteenth to within ten feet of the pin. A roar that could be heard in Atlanta went up. The pines at Augusta National had just stopped vibrating from the blast when Jack dropped his eagle putt, setting off another roar of equal magnitude.

The origin of the first roar at the Masters can be traced back to the cofounder of the Augusta National: Bobby Jones. Jones had retired from the game in 1930 after winning the Grand Slam. He decided before the first Masters in 1934 that he would make a one-time exception to his retirement and compete in the Masters.

Jones's entry in the inaugural tournament created quite a stir, and oddsmakers made him one of the favorites. Attendance on opening day was a trickle by today's standards—only about two thousand patrons were on the grounds at the first Masters, and almost all of them were following the pairing of Jones and Paul Runyan.

Jones's drives and approach shots were as strong as they had been in his glory days, but his short game, especially his putting, was dreadful. At the end of the first round, he had posted a very un–Bobby Jones score of 76. The next day he spent a full hour on the practice green and raised his followers' hopes by rolling in putts from every angle.

Jones again had almost all the Masters patrons present trekking along with him. His play on his full shots was even stronger than the day before, but his putting went further south. Jones missed six putts from four feet or less. The shortest miss was from a foot.

In his glory days, Jones had used his famous putter, Calamity Jane, named after the famous frontierswoman and sharpshooter Martha "Calamity Jane" Canary. Jones needed his Calamity Jane putter now, but she was an ocean away, in the trophy room of the Royal and Ancient Golf Club of St. Andrews, Scotland.

After his poor putting in the second round, Jones remembered that years earlier he had given his mother a Calamity Jane–style putter. Jones placed a call to an Atlanta golf professional, Chuck Ridley. He dispatched Ridley out to the bag room at East Lake Country Club in Atlanta, where his mother's clubs were stored, to get that putter and bring it to him in Augusta.

In that first Masters, the nines were reversed. It was at the par-three thirteenth hole (now the fourth hole) in that third round that the first roar at the Masters boomed out. It was triggered by Jones. He had laced a long iron to about ten feet from the hole. Using his mother's putter, he rolled in the putt for a birdie, and the patrons let loose with the Masters's first huge roar.

Jones would finish the tournament in a tie for thirteenth place. He would play in the Masters through 1948. The 1934 tournament would be his best finish.

AUGUSTA NATIONAL AND EISENHOWER, PART 1

Today a team of Secret Service agents would have this responsibility. But on election night in 1952, the assignment fell to a sixty-year-old investment banker. If central casting had been looking for the perfect fit for the role of a small-town undertaker, this would be the guy: slightly above average height, hawk-nosed, bespectacled, with large ears, his weight just barely out of the undernourished category, and dark thinning hair combed straight back. His appearance and reserved demeanor gave no hint of his power and influence. He was Cliff Roberts, the commander of a very elite group: the membership of the Augusta National Golf Club.

Roberts was standing guard at the door of a room at New York City's Waldorf Astoria Hotel. On the other side of the door, stretched out on a bed catching a few z's, was an Augusta National member who had just won the presidency of the United States in a landslide: General Dwight D. Eisenhower. While they were waiting for Eisenhower's opponent, Adlai Stevenson, to concede, Roberts had ushered the next president of the United States into one of the unoccupied rooms on the Eisenhower campaign's floor so he could get some rest before giving his victory speech.

Roberts's journey to wealth and power began in a small town in America's heartland. He was born in Morning Sun, Iowa. His mother was a distant cousin of Frances Scott Key, the writer of the lyrics to "The Star-Spangled Banner." His father was a real estate salesman who always wanted to see what was on the other side of the next hill, so consequently, the family moved frequently and eventually ended up in Texas.

Roberts never finished high school and took to the road selling men's clothing when he was about sixteen, and he did quite well at it. After several years, he decided New York City was where he needed to make his fortune. After one failed assault on the Big Apple, Roberts regrouped and tried again, but World War I got in the way. He went into the army and ironically received his first exposure to Augusta, Georgia, when he was sent to Fort Hancock, located just outside the city, for basic training. After completing his training, he was shipped over to the war's front in France and served as an ambulance driver.

Following the war, Roberts was able to get a foothold within the New York financial scene, despite his lack of formal education. He endured many ups and downs, including taking a beating in the crash of 1929. He persevered, however, and eventually forged a very successful place for himself on Wall Street, becoming a partner with the prestigious brokerage firm of Reynolds and Company.

In the mid-1920s Roberts took up the game of golf. He soon made it his practice to spend part of the winter in Augusta, Georgia, which at that time was a celebrated retreat for northerners wishing to escape the doldrums of winter and a good place to make business contacts. During those junkets he played golf at the Augusta Country Club and became acquainted with most of the Augusta regulars. When he was introduced to golfing legend Bobby Jones by a mutual acquaintance, the two hit it off quite well, and their long and successful association began.

Roberts became aware of Jones's desire to build his dream course and, while they were both in Augusta during a winter holiday, Roberts put this question to Jones: "Why don't you build that golf course you have been thinking about here in Augusta?" Jones replied, "I will if you will finance it," and a superb partnership was formed.

With Roberts at point, a small but very powerful group of Augusta

National members had provided the key push, both to get Eisenhower into the presidential race and in his campaigns, first for the Republican nomination and then in the general election.

Eisenhower's first encounter with an Augusta National member had, appropriately enough, taken place at a country club, albeit a heavily bombed one. It occurred during World War II, during the Battle of the Bulge. Augusta National member Bill Robinson was the vice president of one of the leading newspapers in the United States, the *New York Herald Tribune*. Before France fell to the Germans, the *Tribune* had published an English-language edition in Paris for ten years.

Soon after the Allies liberated Paris, Robinson arrived there to set the wheels in motion for the *Tribune* to resume publishing its Paris edition. He ran up against some regulations that Eisenhower had imposed concerning the dos and don'ts of doing business in Allied-occupied territory. Robinson requested a meeting with Eisenhower to seek relief from a few of these regulations. The arrangements were worked out for the meeting to take place at Eisenhower's headquarters, which was in the clubhouse of what was left of a war-torn country club near the town of Rheims, northeast of Paris. But a few days before the meeting was to take place, the Battle of the Bulge began. Robinson expected his appointment to be canceled. When he inquired about it, he was told it was still on.

When the meeting began, Robinson apologized to Eisenhower for taking up his time while a big battle was taking place. Eisenhower told him not to worry about it. He was confident that his forces would take care of the situation, and he was now developing plans for action weeks after the current battle. The two men hit it off during the meeting, and they became good friends.

In the spring of 1948, shortly after Eisenhower had retired from the military, Robinson invited Eisenhower down to Augusta National for a golf vacation. There to greet them upon their arrival were the club's cofounders, Jones and Roberts, and two founding members, Robert W. "Bob" Woodruff, the chairman of the Coca-Cola Company, and W. Alton "Pete" Jones, president of the oil and gas giant Cities Service Company (now CITGO).

Soon after the United States entered World War II, Bobby Jones had enlisted in the army and served as an intelligence officer. He had met

Eisenhower in the spring of 1944 in England, during the preparations for the D-Day invasion. Bob Woodruff had already entertained Eisenhower for a weekend soon after the war ended at his plantation at Callaway Gardens near Atlanta.

Eisenhower had done a lot for the Coca-Cola brand during the war. He had pushed for and received portable Coke plants for his troops in Europe. He also gave Coca-Cola one of the biggest free endorsements it ever received. On his initial visit back to the States after Germany's surrender, Eisenhower received an enormous welcome home. His every move was double-covered by the press. At one of his first public appearances, he was asked if there was anything he wanted. He replied, "Could somebody get me a Coke?" One was quickly provided, and after he finished it, he said he had another request: "Another Coke."

Pete Jones, along with Roberts, was meeting Eisenhower for the first time. He had been one of the country's heroes on the home front during World War II, spearheading the construction of an oil pipeline from Texas to the East Coast that was completed in time to support the D-Day invasion. He was also heavily involved with the building of a secret explosive production facility in Arkansas and the construction of an aviation fuel refinery in Louisiana.

Although he had arrived at Augusta National as a guest, Eisenhower departed as a dues-paying member, with Roberts now handling his personal finances. Soon after leaving Augusta, Eisenhower surprised almost everyone when he chose as his first civilian job the presidency of Columbia University. His new job worked out well for his friends from Augusta National as Roberts, Bill Robinson, and Pete Jones were all based in New York City. They got together regularly just outside the city on Wednesday afternoons and Saturdays for golf at Blind Brook Country Club.

AUGUSTA NATIONAL AND EISENHOWER, PART 2

Since D-Day, there had been ongoing talk about an Eisenhower run for president. Being career military, his political leanings were not discernible. Both major political parties were interested in him as a candidate. But as time went by after he left the army, it became clear that Eisenhower's thinking about the direction he believed the country should be taking placed him in line with the Republican Party. There was plenty of excitement about the possibility of him being the party's candidate for president, especially among the members of Augusta National, a GOP stronghold.

In late 1950 President Truman asked Eisenhower to take over command of the North Atlantic Treaty Organization (NATO), headquartered just outside Paris. Eisenhower agreed to take the position and took a leave of absence from Columbia.

Early in January 1951, Eisenhower made a quick trip over to Europe to meet with the leaders of the member nations in NATO. He returned to the States to brief President Truman and Congress on those meetings before officially taking command at the NATO Headquarters later that month. After those briefings, Eisenhower flew to Puerto Rico to have a golf outing with Cliff Roberts and several other Augusta National members before heading back to Paris for his new assignment.

Once at NATO Headquarters, it didn't take long before Eisenhower was a regular on the Paris area golf courses. He did have to adjust one aspect of his golfing. He had always been prone to let the "expletives fly" after a bad shot. Since the caddies in France were almost all female, he made an extreme effort, though not always successful, to keep from having those types of outbursts.

According to logs in the prepresidential files at the Eisenhower Library, Eisenhower played seventy-two rounds of golf during the approximately fourteen months he was in charge of NATO. For a third of those rounds in Paris, a member of Augusta National Golf Club was in the group, stoking the coals in hopes of firing up Eisenhower for a presidential run. Roberts and Bill Robinson made several lengthy visits, while five other Augusta members had shorter stays. Also, Roberts didn't want Eisenhower to feel left out during Masters Week at Augusta National in 1951, so he placed some money down for him in the club's gambling pool and kept him apprised of how his wager was doing by telegram each day.

As the 1952 campaign season began to unfold, Eisenhower seemed to be straddling the fence about whether to enter the race or not. What seemed to tip the scales was when he was shown a film clip of an "Eisenhower for President" rally in Madison Square Garden that drew fifteen thousand enthusiastic supporters. Shortly after seeing the film, Eisenhower threw his hat into the ring.

It appeared at first that Eisenhower may have waited too long to make his decision. Senator Robert Taft of Ohio, the son of former president William Howard Taft, had started his campaigning long before Eisenhower entered the race and appeared to have the inside track for the nomination. But by the time the primary season was over and the two candidates' forces headed to the party's convention the first week of July in Chicago, it was a virtual dead heat.

When he would recall covering the 1952 Republican National Convention, a gleam would return to the eyes of broadcast news legend Walter Cronkite. It was the kind of old-time, no-holds-barred convention that the current news media would give their eye teeth to cover. This epic struggle for the GOP nomination had it all: political rancor, arm-twisting, fisticuffs, backslapping, deals and rumors of deals, and quiet diplomacy.

All of Eisenhower's supporters from Augusta National were committed to the fight. The most dauntless member of the Augusta National Legion was Bobby Jones. Several months after Eisenhower's first Augusta visit, in 1948, Jones had been diagnosed with a spinal disease that would get progressively worse. Now, almost four years later, the effects of the disease had reached the point where he needed a cane to assist him in walking. But Jones was right up on the front lines in the thick of the battle, calling on delegates who were still up for grabs.

Jones's efforts, along with those of the rest of Eisenhower's forces, ultimately won the day. They came up nine votes short of the nomination on the first ballot. Then it was announced that the Minnesota delegation planned to change its nineteen votes to Eisenhower on the second ballot. Since this would give Eisenhower the nomination, other delegations, not wishing to be on the losing side, switched to Eisenhower as well, giving him a huge margin of victory. Two weeks later the Democratic Party held its convention and selected Adlai Stevenson as its nominee.

Because of Roberts's and fellow Augusta National member Alton "Pete" Jones's efforts, funds poured into the Eisenhower campaign for the primaries and the general election—so much so that when the campaign ended, unused funds were returned to contributors.

As the general election campaign unfolded, Eisenhower consistently held a lead of 5 to 7 points in the polls. Six weeks before Election Day, Roberts was so confident of victory that he wrote to the members of Augusta National and advised them their access to the club would be restricted the two weeks immediately following the election. Eisenhower was going to take a working vacation there as soon as the race was over.

When the final vote was tallied, Eisenhower had won 55 to 44 percent, and in the Electoral College the count was Eisenhower 442 and Stevenson 89. Twelve hours after Eisenhower was awakened by Roberts to make his victory speech, a plane chartered by Roberts carrying Eisenhower and his entourage lifted off from New York's LaGuardia Airport headed for Augusta, Georgia. Most of Augusta turned out and lined the streets to cheer Eisenhower as his motorcade made its way from the airport to Augusta National. During his stay Eisenhower spent his mornings working on matters of the transition of power from President Truman's administration to his and spent his afternoons playing golf.

Eisenhower took the Oath of Office on January 20, 1953. His first trip to Augusta National Golf Club as president occurred just over a month after his inauguration. He wrote a letter to Cliff Roberts on February 10, 1953. In the letter he stated he had hoped to get down to Augusta for a long weekend on February 13 but had decided against it. His thinking was it would be bad public relations to take such a trip after being on the job for just three weeks, so he would wait until the second week in April to come down. Only a very limited number of golfers in the country who are capable of satisfying a desire to play Augusta National would know how powerful an urge it must have been. The urge was far too powerful for Eisenhower, a man who had four years earlier kicked a three-pack-a-day cigarette habit, cold turkey. On February 26 Eisenhower's plane streaked down the runway at Andrews Air Force Base outside Washington DC and took to the sky. Its destination: Augusta, Georgia.

"ANYTIME YOU'RE PLAYING WITH ARNOLD THAT HAPPENS"

Forced into a thirty-six-hole final day because of a rain-out on day 1, Arnold Palmer and Jack Nicklaus went at it in a head-to-head duel in the 1970 Byron Nelson Classic in Dallas, Texas, at the Preston Trail Golf Club.

When they teed off in the final group of the day, Nicklaus held the top spot by two strokes over Arnie. Jack would push his lead to four, but Arnie charged back. He had cut the margin to one by the time they reached the tee at the par-four eighteenth, their thirty-sixth hole of the day. Arnie had a chance to win it there when Jack's drive sailed way left and out of the fairway.

Nicklaus's approach failed to find the green, and he could not get up and down. Safely on in two, Arnie just missed on his birdie effort from twenty-one feet, leaving the two players all knotted up for the day.

Arnie and Jack headed back to the 555-yard, par-five fourteenth to begin a sudden-death playoff to settle the matter. Jack outdrove Arnie by 20 yards and was well in range to reach the green in two. Arnie was at a questionable distance. He elected to go with a driver off the deck but came up well short of the green. Jack just missed the green but was pin high. Arnie, afraid of going long, left his short pitch 18 feet below the hole. Jack's chip stopped just 14 inches from the cup. Arnie's putt for birdie rimmed out. Jack tapped in, and it was over.

The vast majority of the fifteen thousand in attendance followed Jack and Arnie throughout the day, and just about all of them were pulling for Palmer. On the thirty-sixth hole, when Jack's drive went awry, cheers went up. Asked about the gallery's partisanship and its effect on him, Nicklaus shrugged it off, saying, "Anytime you're playing with Arnold that happens."

This was the third time the two greats had dueled it out in a playoff. In 1962 they did it at the U.S. Open and at the Western Open in 1963. Both were eighteen-hole playoffs. Nicklaus won at the Open by three strokes. Arnold won at the Western by two.

"BE THE RIGHT CLUB . . . BE THE RIGHT CLUB TODAY!"

In the final round of the Players Championship in 2000, Hal Sutton emphatically exclaimed "Be the right club . . . Be the right club today!" as he watched the six-iron he had just hit as it flew toward the green at the eighteenth hole. The utterance instantly became one of the most memorable ones in the game's history.

It was indeed the right club. It came to rest fifteen feet below the hole and set up Sutton's second victory in the prestigious event, beating the hottest player in golf, Tiger Woods, by one stroke. Woods was in one of the hottest periods of his career. In 1999 he had won eight times, and already in 2000 he had picked up three victories.

Freddie Burns had been Hal's caddie since he went on tour, and before that, he had been Hal's father's caddie at the senior Sutton's country club. Before Hal and Freddie departed for the tour's West Coast swing, which started in mid-January, Hal brought Freddie in for a meeting and told him: "Freddie, somewhere on the West Coast we're going to get paired with Tiger, and I want to make sure that three people know that we can beat him when we have the task. I want you to know it, I want me to know it, and I want him to know it."

At the fifth stop of the West Coast swing at the Nissan Open at the Riveria Country Club in Los Angeles, Hal and Tiger were paired together for the first two rounds. Tiger shot four under par for the two days. Hal was six under.

At the Players, Hal had the lead for the first three rounds. But Tiger was only one stroke behind Hal, and they were paired together for the final round. At the twelfth hole, play was suspended for the rest of the day because of thunderstorms, with Hal holding a three-shot lead. The tournament resumed on Monday. When Hal and Tiger reached the par-five sixteenth tee, Hal was still in the lead by three, but minutes later Tiger turned up the heat. His towering second shot with a three-wood came to rest just a few feet from the hole. Tiger rolled in his eagle putt, and Hal made par. His lead was down to one, with two terrorizing holes remaining, the Island Green seventeenth and the very daunting dogleg left par-four eighteenth.

The seventeenth had already done a number on Hal. He had splashed his tee shot in the third round and made a triple bogey. Woods hit first and cleared the water but didn't quite make the green, ending up in the thick collar of rough on its edge. Hal's shot landed in the middle of the green. He two-putted for a par. Woods had to scramble. He hit a bad chip and had to make a six-footer to save par.

On the eighteenth Woods hit a two-iron to the middle of the fairway. Sutton used his driver and was just a little longer than Tiger. Hitting first and using a six-iron, Tiger's approach was just a little long at the back right of the green.

Hal then pulled out his six-iron. It was a Ben Hogan six-iron. He had a great deal more of a connection to the great Hogan than just using his make of clubs. Many years earlier, Hal's father, a man of considerable means, had secured membership for Hal at Hogan's club, Shady Oaks in Fort Worth, Texas, and Hal had taken personal golf lessons from the great man himself.

Hogan would have been proud of the swing Hal executed that day under tremendous pressure. Years later Hal would tell what was going through his mind as he exclaimed, "Be the right club . . . Be the right club today!" He was sure he had hit the right club, but he was concerned a gust of wind or some other unforeseen occurrence would affect it. That didn't happen.

The shot checked up fifteen feet from the hole. Tiger's chip from off the green for birdie—and to tie Hal—missed by six inches. Hal nestled his first putt up to the hole and then tapped in for par and the win.

His win cooled off Tiger, but not for long. Tiger would win six more times before the end of the year, including the three remaining majors: the U.S. Open, the British Open, and the PGA Championship.

KEEPING YOUR GOLF BALLS FROM GETTING TOO HOT

In 1896 Willie Park Jr., a two-time winner of the British Open, came to the United States to design several golf courses. While here, he took part in a big-money match at the St. Andrew's Golf Club in Yonkers. Park partnered with St. Andrew's member Spalding de Garmendia against the club's golf professional Willie Tucker and another St. Andrew's member, Arthur Livermore. The amount the winning pair would receive was $1,000. That amount would be akin to $35,000 in today's dollars.

The match was played before a large gallery on August 11, one of the hottest days of summer. Park showed up at the first tee carrying a pail that looked like it contained some beverages. But after a few holes, it was observed that the pail contained golf balls packed in ice. The gutta-percha ball in use at that time did not take extreme heat well and would soften up in hot temperatures.

Fearing they had been outsmarted, the team of Tucker and Livermore had supporters take balls to nearby streams to keep them cool. This process didn't work as well as Park's ice pail, but it worked well enough for the team of Tucker and Livermore to win the thirty-six-hole best ball match by three strokes.

About the same time as this big-money match, Coburn Haskell, an executive with a Cleveland, Ohio, mining company, was sitting despondently on his golf club's porch after a bad round. He was twisting a rubber band around his finger while reflecting on his poor play. Haskell was convinced that the gutta-percha ball he had been using that day had been a huge contributor to his bad day on the course. It was made by the B. F. Goodrich Company, at a plant not far from his club. Legend has it that his post-round depression ended when he looked down at the rubber band wrapped around his finger and was struck with a brainstorm: a rubber golf ball.

Haskell contacted a frequent playing partner at the club, Bertram Work, who was employed at B. F. Goodrich in production management, about his idea. Work assisted Haskell in designing the ball, which had a solid rubber core wound in rubber thread. The ball, named the Haskell for its inventor, was much livelier than the gutta-percha, outdistancing it by an average of twenty-five yards.

Haskell and Work obtained a patent for the ball in April 1898. When it went on the market the next year, it faced a substantial amount of resistance. The consensus was that the extra distance a player gained with the Haskell did not offset the difficulty of controlling the lively ball on the green. This resistance faded away in 1901 when Walter J. Travis, considered the best putter in the country, won the U.S. Amateur playing with a Haskell.

Coburn Haskell formed the Haskell Golf Ball Company shortly after Travis's win at the Amateur. Over the next few years, the Haskell ball ended the gutta-percha's nearly half-century reign as the ball of choice.

GOLF AND NUPTIALS

In the winter of 1930, a red flag could have been raised when a young man played twenty-seven holes of golf on the eve of his wedding, then played twenty-seven holes the day after tying the knot and another eighteen holes the next day. But twenty-six-year-old Harry Cooper had a legitimate reason. He was a golf professional participating in the richest golf event ever held.

The event was the Aqua Caliente Open, and the total purse was $25,000, with $10,000 going to the winner. It was being played at a resort course near Tijuana, Mexico, just across the border from San Diego. Rain played havoc with the tournament's planned start date and forced a delay of six days.

The delay threw a wrench into Harry Cooper's plan for matrimony, which had been scheduled for several days after the tournament would have concluded had the rain not intervened. The tournament organizers were sympathetic to Cooper's plight and accommodated him so he could play in the event and keep his wedding plans.

The tournament was to be held over four days, with eighteen holes being played each day. Cooper was allowed to play twenty-seven holes on day 1. He skipped day 2 and traveled the 140 miles to Los Angeles to marry the strikingly beautiful twenty-year-old Emily Buchanan.

Cooper returned to the tournament on day 3 and played twenty-seven holes and then eighteen holes on the last day. He finished the event in thirteenth place and took home $200.

Throughout his career Cooper would win thirty-six tournaments, but he was given the nickname "Hard Luck" for his near misses in the Masters and United States Opens. He was lucky in love. His marriage to Emma lasted for seventy years, until his death at age ninety-six in 2000.

Gene Sarazen won the Aqua Caliente Open by four strokes to take the $10,000 first prize. But he only took home $8,000. Surviving on the tour was tough back in those days even for a player of the stature of Sarazen. Before the tournament, he had agreed with fellow pros Johnny Farrell and Leo Diegel: If one of them won, the winner would give the other $2,000 each.

BURNING TREE CLUB

A Male Bastion

In March 1989 the Maryland Court of Appeals ruled Burning Tree Club, just outside Washington DC in Bethesda, Maryland, would have to give up its long-standing policy of not allowing women on the grounds if it wanted to remain exempt from property taxes. Burning Tree's lawyers appealed the Maryland court's ruling to the United States Supreme Court, which declined to hear the case. At that point Burning Tree decided to maintain the policy of prohibiting women and pay the taxes, which amounted to several hundred thousand dollars a year.

Burning Tree was built in 1922 by four District of Columbia residents who had become frustrated at the long waits to tee off at courses in and around the capital. The course got its name from a tree that once stood at the highest point of the club's property and that had bright-red leaves when it bloomed in the spring.

Since its opening, Burning Tree Club has always been one of the few places in Washington DC where Democrats and Republicans got along. Its members famously included John F. Kennedy, Lyndon Johnson, and Tip O'Neill on the Democratic side, and on the Republican side, George H. W. Bush, Gerald Ford, and Dwight Eisenhower. Admirals, generals,

Supreme Court justices, and high-profile members of the media have also been found on the membership roster.

Well before the court case in 1989, Burning Tree's strict no-women-allowed policy (except on very rare occasions) was well known. In early 1953 club member Prescott Bush, the father of a future president of the United States and the grandfather of another, was put through the wringer in attempting to receive an okay for one of those very rare occasions.

Soon after President Eisenhower was inaugurated, Burning Tree's rigid no-women-allowed policy placed Bush, a United States senator from Connecticut, in a tough spot. He was given a most unenviable assignment. There was to be a dinner in Eisenhower's honor at the club, hosted by the Republicans in the Senate. Bush was assigned to inform Margaret Chase Smith, the Republican senator from Maine, who had been elected to the Senate in 1948, that she would be excluded from the event because of Burning Tree's no-women policy.

Bush protested the assignment and asked the powers that be at Burning Tree to make an exception, but they refused. He swallowed hard and proceeded to carry out the mission in a face-to-face meeting. Bush, recalling the meeting years later, said: "She absolutely hit the ceiling . . . She was simply—furious—furious."

Stung by Smith's blistering reaction to being excluded, Bush went back to the powers that be at Burning Tree and pleaded again for an exception to the rule. Being on the receiving end of Smith's wrath must have sharpened Bush's persuasive skills. He won the appeal. Delighted with himself, he went back to Smith to tell her the good news. Her reaction left Bush with more persuading to do. She told him: "I wouldn't come now for anything! Nobody could make me go!"

Bush pleaded with her to be reasonable and then told her he would pick her up and bring her home and that he had already told Eisenhower she would be sitting on his right at the dinner. Bush admitted later the seating arrangements had not yet been discussed with Eisenhower, but he felt like he needed to use every means at his disposal to win her over. She finally relented and agreed to come.

HE WALKED TO THE BEAT OF A DIFFERENT DRUMMER

Mac O'Grady joined the PGA Tour in 1984, after making it through the qualifying school on his seventeenth attempt. O'Grady was arguably the most eccentric player the tour had ever seen. He contended that he could play just as well left-handed as right-handed and backed it up with numerous demonstrations. His special interest was molecular biology.

But O'Grady's thoughts and how he expressed them really grabbed you and set him apart. Once after a bogey at Pebble Beach, he told a reporter: "I'm going through a catatonic, neurosomatic emotional disorder right now. I'm in total emotional upheaval." His description of a wedge shot was: "a bird flying to the firmaments, outlined against an incandescent sky, beginning to fall, gently sashaying back to the earth."

There was a flip side to O'Grady, as he could be volatile and was the first to admit to being his own worst enemy. He had a strong aversion to authority, especially the authority of PGA commissioner Deane Beman and his management of the tour. His tirades about Beman that appeared in print resulted in him being suspended from the tour in 1986 for six events, for conduct unbecoming a professional golfer.

O'Grady appealed his suspension, first to Beman, who rejected it, and then to his court of last resort, the PGA Tour's three-member Appeals Committee. While the appeals process was running its course, O'Grady continued to compete. In the Canon Sammy Davis Jr.–Greater Hartford Open, he shot a final-round 62 and then beat Roger Maltbie on the first hole of a playoff to record the first of his two wins on tour.

At the awards presentation ceremony, O'Grady said, "There are times when you spread your wings and your molecules rise higher than they ever had before." He then added, "For the dreamers of the world, the people whose spirits have been fragmented along the yellow brick road, this day I share with them."

Shortly after his win at Hartford, the Appeals Committee upheld O'Grady's suspension. After his suspension, he continued to make headlines by his words and actions. The most publicized of these was a physical brawl outside the scorer's tent at the Federal Express St. Jude Open in Memphis in 1989, with the father of the caddie who had carried his bag the day before.

O'Grady left the tour in 1990 because of an issue with his spine, and he became a top-flight golf instructor, opening a school in Palm Springs and working with some of the tour's top names.

IT WOULD HAVE BEEN A GREAT STORY

Lee Westwood, a native of Worksop, Nottinghamshire, England, had a lot on the line as he played the finishing holes of the 2009 British Open at the Turnberry Golf Club. After eighteen tournament wins all over the world, he stood a very good chance of finally winning a major. To make things even more interesting, his sponsor had pledged to give him a $2 million bonus for a British Open win.

Westwood had taken the lead at the seventh hole with an eagle. He held or shared it for most of the round, but bogeys at three of the last four holes, including a three-putt on eighteen, ended his chances and dropped him to one under, one stroke behind clubhouse leader Stewart Cink, who had rolled in a fifteen-foot putt for birdie at the eighteenth to move to two under. But coming down the finishing holes behind Westwood was a player who stood a very good chance of bettering Cink's total and in doing so making an incredible entry in golf history. The player was fifty-nine-year-old Tom Watson.

During the first two rounds, Watson's surprisingly strong score had been the feel-good story of the tournament, but the consensus was that at his age there was no way he could keep it up over the remaining two rounds. The oldest player to win a major to this point had been Julius Boros. He won the 1968 PGA Championship at the age of forty-eight. But Watson put plenty of doubt into the minds of the consensus when the third round ended; he was in sole possession of the lead by one stroke.

It looked like the consensus would be proved right, however, because as the final round got underway, Watson stumbled out of the gate. When he reached the fourth tee, he had lost the lead. But he hung on and took the lead back with a birdie at the par-five seventeenth.

History was on Watson's side as he teed it up at eighteen—the hole had been good to him. Each hole at Turnberry had a name. The eighteenth's original name was Ailsa Hame, but over time that changed. After Watson outdueled Jack Nicklaus in the Open at Turnberry in 1977, the contest became known as the "Duel in the Sun"—from a late 1940s western film starring Gregory Peck. One of the taglines for the film described it as an "unparallel spectacle of thrills." Some years later, the eighteenth hole at Turnberry would be renamed "Duel in the Sun."

The duel between Nicklaus and Watson certainly lived up to the name. The two had separated themselves from the field and were paired together for the final two rounds. In the third round they both shot 65. In the final round it came down to the last two holes. Watson birdied seventeen, and Nicklaus missed a knee knocker for birdie and tapped in for par, and Watson was in the lead by one.

At the par-four eighteenth, Watson hit an iron off the tee, and he was in good shape in the fairway. Nicklaus unleashed a driver; it carried past Watson's ball, but it was wildly off line and ended up in thick rough. Watson hit a superb approach to within two feet of the hole. Nicklaus lashed out of the rough to the front of the green some forty feet from the cup. He made Watson's putt just a little longer when his birdie putt dropped into the heart of the cup. But Watson handled the pressure and rolled his putt in for birdie to capture the victory.

In 2009, at the eighteenth, Watson hit a solid tee shot, but his approach was just a little long and missed the green. He elected to try and get up and down with his putter. His putt from off the green stopped rolling seven feet from the hole. His par putt for the win was that of a high-handicap weekend golfer. It was weak and offline. He tapped in for par.

In the four-hole playoff with Cink, Watson suddenly looked drained. Father time had finally caught up with him. He fell one behind after the first hole and matched Cink at the second. But at the third playoff hole, the seventeenth, he made a double bogey to Cink's birdie, making the play of the last playoff hole just a formality.

In his post-tournament press conference, Watson said: "In my profession, when you have a chance to win the World Open, as I call it, and you give it away . . . it tears your guts out . . . It would have been a great story."

SUNDAY GOLF

As golf was getting a foothold in the United States, it was taken up almost exclusively by the rich and was consequently regarded by "average Americans" with an air of contemptuousness, as the sports and whims of their wealthy fellow countrymen were commonly viewed. The strongest attacks against golf were coming from the pulpit.

Restrictions on the activities of the populace on Sunday in the United States had first been enacted in New Haven, Connecticut, in the late seventeenth century. Eventually, they were on the books in all the colonies. These statutes were called "blue laws."

The early golfers at St. Andrew's in Yonkers were laughed at for playing their odd game on Saturday. And on Sunday they would be scorned for taking part in such an activity on the day that was set aside for worship and rest. As the game grew in the country, so did the criticism of it being played on Sunday. Arrests for breaking the blue laws by golfing on Sunday were commonplace each spring and summer. The New York City area typically led the way in arrests, followed by New Jersey and Connecticut. Many were also jailed in Philadelphia, and one time in Boston, nine

Harvard students found themselves behind bars for teeing it up on a Sunday morning.

In the late spring of 1901 the tipping point for golfing on Sunday would, coincidentally, take place where the game got its first real foothold in this country: Yonkers, New York. That spring ministers of several denominations in the New York City area marshaled their forces and launched an aggressive campaign against Sunday golf. They petitioned local law enforcement agencies to rigorously enforce the blue laws that were on the books. After exerting pressure on law enforcement, the ministers in unison used their sermons to condemn Sunday golf.

The following week the controversy over Sunday golf continued to heat up. A number of wealthy golfers threatened to leave their churches unless the agitation against Sunday golf was stopped, while police officials announced they would be rigorously enforcing the blue laws in the future. It came to a boil the next Sunday in Yonkers.

The Saegkill Golf Club in Yonkers had opened the year before. Benjamin Adams, a prominent attorney and a member of the school board, was playing the course that Sunday, while two female friends and a male friend walked along with him. Adams was well into his round when two detectives of the Yonkers Police Department marched up to the group and placed Adams under arrest and hauled him off to jail. He was bailed out in short order.

The following day Adams was arraigned in superior court. The usual occurrence in a blue law violation case would be that at arraignment the accused would plead guilty and pay a fine. But Adams would have none of that. He requested a trial by jury. His request was granted, and the trial was set for three days later.

Adams's trial was great theater. The courtroom at city hall, a former manor house built in 1658, was packed with spectators on both sides of the issue. Adams's case would be decided by a six-man jury, and the deck appeared to be stacked against him. The district attorney's office had elected not to assign a prosecutor to the case, which meant the judge, the Honorable William C. Kellogg, would also serve in a dual role in the proceedings: prosecutor and judge. Adams was being defended by a battery of fellow lawyers, with his lead counsel being Joseph F. Daly.

The fireworks in the case started during the jury selection process. In the jury pool was a Mr. Jay Bell. And when his name was called to be seated as the sixth and final juror, he rose and walked confidently to the jury box, while the spectators in the courtroom gasped and giggled. Mr. Bell's attire immediately identified him as being a problem for the prosecution. Since the forming of the Royal and Ancient Golf Club of St. Andrews, members of golf clubs wore special colorful jackets that identified them with that particular club. These jackets were worn on special days at the club and during competitions against other golf clubs. Mr. Bell was wearing the bright-red golf jacket with matching knickers worn by the members of the Saegkill Golf Club.

When Mr. Bell took his seat in the jury box, he looked over at Adams and his attorneys and winked. Judge Kellogg immediately excused him from jury service. Mr. Daly objected. He insisted on the right to have him, and this triggered a series of heated exchanges between him and Judge Kellogg, before the judge upheld his decision to excuse Mr. Bell. Another juror was called, and the trial began.

The prosecution called only one witness, one of the arresting officers, Detective Welsh. He provided his accounts of the previous Sunday. How he had found Mr. Adams, clad in a red coat, smashing a white ball around at the Saegkill Golf Club. During his cross-examination, Mr. Daley got Detective Welsh to testify that golf was a quiet game, that Mr. Adams had not been causing a public disturbance, and that he was on private property when he was arrested. The only witness for the defense was the president of the Saegkill Golf Club. He testified that the club was duly incorporated and in control of the grounds where the arrest occurred.

Citing the individual liberty and religious freedom guaranteed by the U.S. Constitution, Mr. Daly made an impassioned summation to the jury on behalf of his client. Judge Kellogg then charged the jury. He first read the blue law statute. He then instructed the jury that it was their duty to decide the case according to the law on the books and that the defendant was being charged with willfully breaking that law. A juror interrupted the judge at one point and asked if the fact that the offense had taken place on private property should have any bearing on the case. "None whatsoever," replied Judge Kellogg. At this point Mr. Daly rose and made the motion that the jury be instructed to decide the case according to their consciences. Judge Kellogg denied the motion.

The jury deliberated for forty-five minutes. When they returned to the courtroom, Judge Kellogg asked for the verdict. The foreman rose and read it: "We, the jury, find the defendant, Adams, not guilty, and we recommend that the existing law in regard to the Observance of the Sabbath on the first day of the week be repealed or amended so as to not to interfere with the innocent amusement of the citizens of this State on that day."

The verdict in Yonkers was the turning point for Sunday golf in the Northeast. But as the game spread and grew in popularity, Sunday golf would continue to be a hot-button issue for the next three decades in other parts of the country.

A BLESSED FINAL ROUND?

As the last day of the 1956 Masters began, it appeared that by the end of the day, it would conclude with one of the biggest stories ever in golf: an amateur, Ken Venturi, was going to be the winner. But it was not to be.

This Masters was played in the most brutal weather conditions in the event's history, with cold temperatures and vicious winds that made the fairways feel like wind tunnels. Venturi had handled the conditions better than anybody in the first three rounds, having the lead after each day's play concluded.

But on Sunday it was a different story. Twenty-nine players shot 80 or better, and Venturi would be in that number. When the day began, he was in the lead by four strokes over second place's Cary Middlecoff and five strokes ahead of third place's Doug Ford.

Two players were eight shots behind, in a tie for the fourth spot: Lloyd Mangrum, winner of the 1946 United States Open, and Jackie Burke Jr., a five-time winner on the PGA Tour. Burke surmised he had no real chance of catching Venturi and set his sights on outplaying Middlecoff for second place. From a financial standpoint, with Venturi being an amateur, the second-place finisher would receive the first-place check.

Middlecoff started red-hot, birdieing the first two holes, but starting at the fourth hole, he began having putting problems that would last for the remainder of the round, and Burke soon was ahead of him.

Venturi was steady for the first seven holes, making all pars, but a bogey at the eighth hole started him on a downhill slide that would see him bogey eight of the last eleven holes.

Burke, playing ahead of Venturi, made a critical birdie at the seventeenth hole to pull even with Venturi at one over par. He parred eighteen for a score of 71, and then, when Venturi bogeyed the eighteenth to finish with a score of 80, the green jacket was his.

It was indeed a remarkable Masters Sunday. It was made even more remarkable by the fact that Burke had had very little warm-up time before the round. He had opted to go to church instead.

BOBBY JONES GOES HOLLYWOOD

In January 1931 Hollywood's Lakeside Golf Club member George Marshall traveled across the country to visit Bobby Jones in his hometown of Atlanta. On the first full day of his visit, Marshall played a round of golf with Jones at his home course: the East Lake Golf Club. At the time Marshall had an eight handicap. But on that day he played like a pro on the front nine, shooting a three-under-par 33. The wind kicked up on the back nine, and Marshall cooled off a bit, shooting a 42. But his 75, on a course he had never seen before, was still five strokes better than his handicap. Marshall attributed his stellar front nine and his solid showing overall to having Jones as a playing partner. He told a reporter after the round: "You know it's amazing how simply watching that boy's smooth effortless methods inspires a fellow to shoot golf."

Exposing many of the nation's golfers to Jones's methods was what had brought Marshall to Atlanta. In 1930, shortly after completing his Grand Slam and retiring from competitive golf, Jones signed a contract with Warner Brothers to make a series of golf instructional films. Marshall was a film director for Warner Brothers at that time and was assigned the Jones project. His trip to Atlanta was to lay the foundation for the production of the series, which was to begin in Hollywood approximately six weeks later.

For a career that spanned all or parts of seven decades, George Marshall was one of the most prolific directors in Hollywood history. Hired as an extra at Universal Studios in 1912, Marshall became a bit player, prop boy, makeup man, film editor, cameraman, and director successively. He made a smooth transition from silent films to sound. Among his credits on the big screen were *You Can't Cheat an Honest Man*, starring W. C. Fields; *Destry Rides Again*, starring Jimmy Stewart; and *Houdini*, starring Tony Curtis. The Jones series would be titled *How I Play Golf* and would explain the methods Jones employed on the course from tee to green, focusing on certain fundamentals he believed were the same for all golfers. In the series Marshall did not merely want to have Jones stand in front of the camera and announce he was going to play a drive and then merely play the same and go on and explain the process. Marshall wanted "human interest." He decided, with Jones's consent, to give each segment its own storyline, which would include Jones giving the actors who were playing average golfers in the segment instruction on that episode's topic.

Finding actors to portray average golfers or have supporting roles was not a problem as some of the biggest names in Hollywood volunteered their services free of charge. Warner Brothers initially wanted only actors currently under contract to their studio to appear in the series, but the company soon had a change of heart and let stars from other studios have roles as well. This gave the series the most celebrated cast in the history of short subjects. It included Edward G. Robinson, Loretta Young, James Cagney, Joan Blondell, Walter Huston, and Douglas Fairbanks Jr.

The series consisted of twelve ten-minute episodes. It started with the putter and worked up through the short iron, long irons, and woods. Each installment had a storyline but no script. Marshall allowed the stars and Jones to wing their way through each episode. The result was what many believe to be the best sports instruction series ever produced.

A MEMBER OF THE UNITED STATES' ATOMIC TEAM AIDS PRESIDENT EISENHOWER'S GAME

Eight years after the end of World War II, two of the men portrayed in the 2023 movie *Oppenheimer* came to the aid of the president of the United States, Dwight D. Eisenhower, by getting into his hands a device that would assist him with an activity that he was very passionate about: his golf game.

When Eisenhower became a member of the Augusta National Golf Club, he went all in on golf. He practiced or played at every opportunity and was always seeking ways to improve his game.

The event that led Eisenhower to receive the device was an evening at the opera in the spring of 1953 in Washington DC. During an intermission Lewis Strauss, the chairman of the Atomic Energy Commission, who was portrayed by the Oscar-nominated Robert Downey Jr. in *Oppenheimer*, had a conversation with Eisenhower. Strauss informed Eisenhower of the device developed by Luis Alvarez, one of the country's top scientific minds. In short order one of the devices was on the way to the White House.

Before joining Robert Oppenheimer's team at Los Alamos, in 1943, Alvarez, portrayed by Alex Wolff in the film, had already made significant contributions to the war effort. He had developed a device for submarine-hunting aircraft. It would deceive enemy radar operators into believing an aircraft was going away from them instead of heading their direction. He also developed a system that allowed ground-based operators to use precision to guide planes in for a landing during bad weather.

Alvarez's first assignment at Los Alamos was to come up with a means of determining how far along the Germans were in their atomic program. He devised a plan that would have planes carrying a system to detect the radioactive gases produced by a nuclear reactor fly over Germany.

The plan was implemented. No gases were detected as the German program had not yet been successful in developing an operational nuclear reactor. After that, Alvarez's assignment moved from detection to detonation.

By this time the work on Little Boy, the uranium bomb that would be dropped on Hiroshima, was already far along. Alvarez was assigned to the team working on Fat Man, the plutonium bomb that would be dropped on Nagasaki. It required a much more intricate detonation system, which Alvarez would develop, than the one for Little Boy.

Although Alvarez did not work on Little Boy, he did get to see it used. The Hiroshima bomb drop mission consisted of three planes: the *Enola Gay*, which carried Little Boy; the *Great Artiste*, equipped with instrumentation to measure the effects of the bomb; and *Necessary Evil*, which carried scientific observers and cameras. Alvarez was aboard *Necessary Evil*.

After the war Alvarez returned to his American experimental physicist and professor post at the University of California at Berkeley. After World War II he would go on to file seventeen patents. Sixteen of these patents were over a far-reaching range of scientific areas, and one, the first that he filed, was for the golf device.

Alvarez's passion for golf was on par with President Eisenhower's. The golf device was given the name "Stroboscopic Golf Training Device." It used bright flashes of light to illuminate the club position at five points during the downswing. This allowed the user to determine whether the clubhead was on the proper path to the ball, so tendencies to hit a hook or slice could be corrected. It was also equipped with a timing device that measured the speed of the swing.

In 1968 Alvarez was awarded the Nobel Prize in Physics for his work in particle physics.

THE GOLDEN BEAR AND INVERRARY

The Inverrary Golf Club in Lauderhill, Florida, was very good to Jack Nicklaus. Before the Players Championship found its permanent home in Ponte Vedra Beach, Florida, the event was played at three different sites during its first three years of existence, the Atlanta Country Club in 1974, the Colonial Country Club in Fort Worth in 1975, and at Inverrary in 1976. Nicklaus won at Inverrary by three strokes.

In 1977 Inverrary returned to hosting its regular event on the PGA Tour, the Jackie Gleason Inverrary Classic. Nicklaus won in a runaway by five strokes.

In the 1978 edition of the event, it appeared that Nicklaus's run was over. He opened with a two-under-par 70 but slipped well back into the pack with a 75 in the second round. Nicklaus turned it on in the third round with a fabulous 66 to move in on the leaders. In the final round, when he stood over a chip shot eighty feet from the hole at the fourteenth green, he was three strokes behind the front-runner, his playing partner, Grier Jones. Using a three-iron, he perfectly executed a bump-and-run shot that dropped into the hole for birdie.

Nicklaus rolled in a twelve-footer on number fifteen for another birdie, but Jones answered with a birdie to stay two shots ahead. At sixteen Nicklaus chipped in from eighteen feet with a nine-iron to pull within one. At seventeen he rolled in a twenty-foot birdie putt to pull even with Jones. At eighteen he stuck a nine-iron approach within four feet. Jones made par, and Nicklaus rolled in his birdie putt to win by one.

In speaking with the press afterward, Nicklaus said: "I got myself on a roll—it's happened to me a number of times in my career . . . You get on a roll, and you just keep going. Sometimes you don't realize you're on a roll until it's over."

TWO FORMER PRODIGIES BATTLE IT OUT IN A PLAYOFF

Billy Mayfair and Tiger Woods had both been much-heralded teen prodigies—Mayfair in the early eighties and Tiger in the early nineties. The two battled each other in a playoff in March 1998 at the Nissan Open at the Valencia Country Club near Los Angeles.

Before the tournament, Mayfair, who had turned pro in 1988, had recorded three victories to date. His last win had come in 1995, and there were lingering thoughts in the back of his mind if he would ever win again. On the other hand, Tiger, who had turned pro in the late summer of 1996, was on a roll. He had already won six times, including a Masters title.

In the final round, Mayfair was tied with Tiger Woods for the lead when he teed off on the par-five eighteenth hole. But as he waited to hit his second shot, Tiger Woods, up on the green, let out a yell and did a rendition of his signature fist pump. He had drained a fifteen-footer for birdie to take the lead.

Mayfair took a deep breath and pulled out his three-wood for his second shot. The shot strayed to the right and landed in a greenside bunker. Billy then executed a splendid bunker shot that came to rest just inside five feet. With Woods and a huge gallery frozen in silence, Billy rolled in his putt for birdie to force a playoff.

Billy and Tiger then headed back to the eighteenth's tee box. With the hole measuring 565 yards, Tiger's super length gave him the clear advantage. But Tiger lost his drive to the right, and it strayed into the rough. Tiger could not reach the green with his second shot, coming up 30 yards short. Billy, after hitting the fairway, laid up 85 yards from the hole. He then put the pressure on Tiger with a beautiful sand wedge shot that landed about nine feet above the hole and then spun back to five feet below the cup.

Tiger hit his third too strong, and his putt for birdie just slipped by the hole from fifteen feet. Billy, who had not birdied the hole in the first three rounds, calmly duplicated his birdie putt of twenty-five minutes earlier, and the crowd let out a huge roar.

As of this writing, Tiger has been in eleven playoffs on the PGA Tour. The one against Mayfair is the only one he lost.

GOLF PLAYS A HUGE ROLE IN THE FIRST GIGANTIC CORPORATE DEAL

Renowned golf course architect Donald Ross designed such famed courses as Pinehurst No. 2, Oak Hill, Inverness, Scioto, and East Lake Golf Club. His designs have hosted U.S. Opens, Ryder Cups, and PGA Championships.

In 1917 Ross designed a private nine-hole course on the Pennsylvania estate of Charles Schwab, an enormously wealthy steel magnate. Schwab and his play of the game just reached the casual player category. Having a private course for him was just another bauble. He had been living very large for the last sixteen years as a result of a business deal he had orchestrated. And a round of golf had played a big role in pulling it off.

In 1901 the thirty-nine-year-old Schwab was the chief executive of Andrew Carnegie's steel empire. Twenty-two years earlier, he had begun working for the company on the floor of one of its mills for one dollar a day. He soon worked his way into management, and a star was born. He progressed rapidly through several posts, and in 1897 he became president of Carnegie Steel.

In December 1900 Schwab was invited to give a speech on the prospects of the steel industry at a gathering of financial key players in New

York City, at the University Club on Fifth Avenue. Sitting next to the lectern was a man well known as "no easy sell," corporate financier and Wall Street kingpin J. P. Morgan. Schwab's speech ran long, very long, but he held his audience in rapt attention—especially Morgan, who was so engrossed that he never fired up his trademark cigar. After Schwab concluded his speech, Morgan took him aside for further discussions on the steel industry. The conversation lasted an hour.

Two weeks later Morgan sent word to Schwab through an intermediary that he would like to purchase Carnegie Steel, and he wanted Schwab to serve as his go-between. Morgan indicated he would make it well worth Schwab's while, but this was a dicey proposition. Carnegie had a disdain for bankers and Wall Street players. Over the last several years, he had developed a particular disdain for Morgan, especially as he had put together the financial backing of a new competitor to Carnegie Steel, the Federal Steel Company.

Schwab agreed to a covert meeting with Morgan and several of his backers on a Sunday night in Morgan's library. After the meeting Schwab, who had garnered a well-earned reputation as a risk-taker, went all in.

Schwab had an ace in the hole: Carnegie's wife, Louise. He knew she had wanted her husband to retire for some time, and Schwab decided to enlist her aid. Louise went all in as well. And she suggested a golf outing at St. Andrew's Golf Club to loosen up her husband before Schwab made his pitch. Schwab took her advice.

On a cold January afternoon in 1901, Schwab and Carnegie bundled up and made the trek out from Carnegie's New York City mansion to Westchester in an open car to play a round at St. Andrew's. After the round the two retired to Carnegie's fairway cottage for hot drinks and a bite of food.

Schwab was well aware of Carnegie's desire to use most of the great wealth he had gained for philanthropic purposes. He opened his pitch by reviewing Carnegie's desires toward that end. And then Schwab advised him that with that goal in mind, the time had come to put his assets in liquid form. Schwab then revealed his talks with Morgan and that Morgan was prepared to buy him out.

In recalling that afternoon some years later, Schwab said that Carnegie's eyes glazed over, and he looked out the window at the golf course for some time and then turned to him and said yes to the deal. Schwab asked for a price. On a slip of paper, Carnegie wrote in pencil, "$400 million." Morgan took the offer without any haggling. Schwab's take from the deal was later reported to be $25 million.

After the sale Carnegie went to work giving away most of his fortune to worthy endeavors and golfing. In a chance encounter with Morgan sometime later, Carnegie lamented to Morgan that he should have asked for more in the deal—to which Morgan replied, "I would have paid it."

BEN IS BACK

In late March 1949, seven weeks after Ben Hogan's horrific late-night crash on a lonely stretch of Texas highway, it was announced that he was well enough to be released from the El Paso, Texas hospital and would be returning to his Fort Worth home.

The accident occurred as Ben and his wife, Valerie, were returning home after his play in the Phoenix Open. A Greyhound bus attempting to pass a truck pulled directly into the path of Hogan's brand-new Cadillac. All Ben had time to do was to hurl his body across the seat to shield his wife during the impact. It was a move that saved his own life, as the impact drove the steering column into the rear section of the car. Thanks to Ben, Valerie received only minor injuries, but Ben was in bad shape. He had suffered a broken collarbone, fractured ribs, a complex pelvic fracture, facial and eye injuries, a fractured left ankle, and damage to his left leg.

The prognosis for Ben to recover and return to his golf career did not look good—three weeks after he entered the hospital, an internationally known surgeon had to be brought in to perform surgery to reduce the possibility of blood clots reaching Ben's heart. When he was finally well enough to talk to reporters, they were told by Ben's brother not to ask questions about when he would return to golf.

After his return to his Fort Worth home, his recovery was painfully slow, but through extensive walking, he grew steadily stronger. His return to golf came at the LA Open, eleven months after the accident. It was quite a return. Ben finished second, losing in a playoff to Sam Snead.

MR. ICICLE

In 1973 Lloyd Mangrum passed away from a heart attack, with his wife of thirty-five years, Elita, by his side. Mangrum, the 1946 United States Open winner, had not left this world without a fight. The heart attack was his twelfth.

With a pencil-thin mustache and his dark hair parted in the middle, the slender Mangrum looked the part of a riverboat gambler—more times than not when he played a shot, a cigarette was dangling from his lips. His fellow players nicknamed him "Mr. Icicle."

Born in Texas, Mangrum's family relocated to Southern California when he was a teen. Mangrum never played amateur golf and never took lessons. Like many other golfers of that era, he started in golf as a caddie. On his first attempt at making it on the PGA Tour, he went belly up, but not before engaging in what would be a long-standing feud with one of the biggest names in the game: Gene Sarazen.

At one of those tournaments in Mangrum's first attempt to make it on tour, Sarazen was in the group behind Mangrum's and twice drove into his group on the front nine. The pace of the group ahead of Mangrum's was slow, and he and his group were waiting to drive on the tenth tee when

Sarazen's group caught up with them. Sarazen sat down on a bench and told Mangrum and his group to "get moving."

Mangrum turned to face Sarazen and said: "Mr. Sarazen, you'll probably win this tournament. I'm trying to make one hundred dollars to get out of town on. But if you play into me again, I'm gonna take your #$%@! ball and hit it back over your #$%@! head."

Back home flat busted, Mangrum, with the support of his wife, who operated a beauty salon, and the money he racked up hustling on local courses, he put together enough funds to make another run at it on tour, and it paid off.

Mangrum won on tour five times before being inducted into the U.S. Army in 1942. His unit was in training for the D-Day landing when he was offered the golf professional position at the army's Fort Meade golf course in Maryland, but he declined.

In combat he was injured when his jeep overturned; he sustained a broken elbow. Later he would be shot in the knee by a German sniper. He was awarded a Purple Heart, two Silver Stars, and two Bronze Stars.

Six months after being discharged from the army, Mangrum won the 1946 United States Open at the Canterbury Golf Club outside Cleveland, Ohio. He was tied with Byron Nelson and Vic Ghezzi after seventy-two holes. There was a thirty-six-hole playoff the next day, with Mangrum posting a score of 144, while Nelson's and Ghezzi's totals were 145.

Mangrum would win thirty more times on tour. Four of those wins came at the Los Angeles Open. In 1953 he captained the United States team to victory in the Ryder Cup at the Wentworth Club west of London.

After his U.S. Open win in 1946, he said that moment was the second happiest of his life. The first had been in the hospital when he was recuperating from the broken elbow he sustained when his jeep overturned. He was concerned that his golf career might be over. His doctor told him that once his cast was off, if he could raise his elbow over his head, he would be able to swing a golf club again.

When the cast came off, he slowly raised his elbow over his head without a problem, and that was, without a doubt, the happiest moment of his life.

A BAD LOOK FOR BUBBA

There's no other way to say it. It was a bad look for Bubba Watson. It happened in the final round of the 2013 Travelers Championship in Hartford, Connecticut. Bubba was caught in a moment of disappointment and exploded in a verbal tirade, displaying the attitude of a first-class jerk.

The target of Bubba's wrath was his caddie, Ted Scott. The two were in their seventh year together, and this was undoubtedly the low point of their player-caddie relationship.

The tirade occurred after Bubba, who was in the lead, hit his tee shot at the par-three sixteenth. The shot was a forced carry over water. His tee shot caught the bank in front of the green and rolled back into the water.

Bubba then ripped into Ted over his recommendation for the club Bubba had used. As he played the rest of the hole, Bubba kept firing barbs at Ted. Bubba finished the hole with a triple-bogey six. The triple bogey cost Bubba the tournament.

The tirade Bubba unleashed on Ted had been seen in its entirety on CBS's telecast. Before the sun went down, the hashtag "prayforTedScott" was trending big on Twitter.

Ted took full responsibility for what happened at sixteen, saying Bubba wanted to hit an eight-iron and he talked him into a nine. "I convinced him to hit the wrong club," Ted said. "I one hundred percent take responsibility for it. It's totally my fault."

Ted went on later to say, "Yeah, Hartford wasn't a good scenario, and it hurt his public image, but if I had a camera that followed me around all the time to catch when I might be honking at someone on the road or having a bad day and say something I shouldn't have, it doesn't mean I'm a bad person."

In 2006 Ben Crane, one of Bubba's Bible study companions, was responsible for hooking up Bubba with Ted. Bubba was looking for a like-minded Christian to be on his bag, and Crane recommended Ted, who had tried professional golf as a player briefly and had a couple of years of caddying under his belt on the PGA Tour.

Bubba and Ted would put the Travelers incident behind them and stay together for another eight years. They parted company amicably in October 2021, at Bubba's request. Bubba was unsure what the future held for him and believed Ted should pursue other options. Their record together over fifteen years was twelve victories, including the Masters in 2012 and 2014.

Sometime in November 2021, another player asked Ted to be his caddie. The player was Scottie Scheffler. The two had met in a Bible study, so Scottie told Ted and his family to pray on it for a week. After two weeks of prayers, Ted's family felt it was the right decision for him to take Scottie's bag.

But before Ted officially agreed to be Scottie's caddie, he had a question for him. Scheffler had a reputation for getting angry on the course and sometimes directing that frustration toward his caddie. Ted wanted him to work on eliminating that behavior. And Scottie said yes.

The rest, as they say, is history. And it is quite a history. As of this writing, with Ted on his bag, Scottie has won seventeen times on the PGA Tour, including four majors and two Players Championships.

THE SCHENECTADY PUTTER

Born in a Bonfire

In 1901, at an outdoor party where people were socializing seated around a bonfire in the late evening in Schenectady, New York, Arthur F. "Frank" Knight, an engineer at the local General Electric Plant, drew the assignment of stoking the fire. Given that no implements were handy for this purpose, the young engineer had to improvise. So he found a metal shaft from an old umbrella to prod the fire.

Ever since the first golf clubs were developed, the shaft of the putter had always been joined to its head on the near side of the club. During one of his prods of the bonfire that evening, the umbrella's tip pierced a blackened ember about the size of the head of a putter. When Knight, an avid golfer, brought the shaft up from the fire with the ember on its tip, he discovered he had pierced it almost dead in its center. He looked at it momentarily and then laughingly proclaimed he had found a new design for a putter. A few days later, he put that design on paper. He began working on the prototype in the shed behind his house, and by the spring of 1902, he had perfected it.

Golf course architect Devereux Emmet, who designed numerous courses in New York State, New England, and the Congressional Country Club in Washington DC, happened to be in Schenectady doing some follow-up work on a course he had designed. Knight took his new style putter to show him. Emmet asked to borrow the putter so he could take it back to his home course, where he proposed to "play with it" and show it to some of his fellow members. Emmet's home course, which he also designed, was the Garden City Golf Club. One of the members Emmet showed the "Schenectady" was Walter Travis.

In November 1896 Van Cortlandt Golf Course in the Bronx, New York, played host to the first tournament ever held at a public golf course in America. The event was open only to golfers who were not members of a club in the United States Golf Association. John Reid, president of the St. Andrew's Club in Yonkers, served as referee for the tournament. The members of St. Andrew's had chipped in to provide the silver cup for the winner. Thirty-five golfers competed.

Walter Travis finished in sixth place that day. The thirty-five-year-old Travis had only taken up the game that summer, but in just a few short years, he would become the biggest name in golf in America.

Travis hailed from Australia. He arrived in the States in 1885, when his employer, a hardware concern, picked him to head up their New York City office. Eleven years later, he moved to England for about a year and became interested in golf but never actually played the game. He returned to the United States in the summer of 1896. Shortly before he left England, Travis purchased a set of golf clubs, and upon his return, he joined the Oakland Golf Club on Long Island, where he played or practiced at every opportunity.

In 1898 Travis entered the U.S. Amateur at the Morristown Country Club in Morristown, New Jersey. In a huge surprise in the match play event, he stormed his way into the semifinals before falling. The following year he again played in the event, before again losing in the semifinals. But in 1900 and 1901 he won the event, making him the biggest name in USA Golf.

Travis's age and the fact that he played most of his shots with a cigar in his mouth prompted his younger competitors to start referring to him as "the Old Man." The nickname would stick to Travis like the "Golden Bear" moniker would stick to Jack Nicklaus many decades later.

Within forty-eight hours of Travis holding Frank Knight's putter for the first time, he sent a telegram to Knight ordering a putter like Mr. Emmet's. Knight wasted no time in sending one to Travis. A short time later, Travis, the acknowledged best putter in the country, declared that Knight's putter was "the best putter I have ever used."

Travis did not receive Knight's putter until after the 1902 U.S. Amateur. His attempt to win that championship for the third straight year came up short when he was eliminated in the quarterfinal round. The first time Travis used his new putter in competition came later that year, in early October, in the United States Open. The site for the Open was Travis's Garden City Club. He and twelve other amateurs joined eighty professionals in the field. Travis putted brilliantly with his new putter and finished the contest in a tie for second place.

Thanks to the buzz about Travis's new putter at the U.S. Open, within a week of its conclusion Knight had received over one hundred requests for a putter like Travis's. He immediately geared up to go into large-scale production, but Knight had a problem. His putter didn't have a name, or so he thought. He arranged a meeting with Devereux Emmet and Travis. In the meeting he sought permission to name it the "Travis Putter." But both Travis and Emmet disagreed with that idea. Both of them had consistently referred to it as the "Schenectady Putter" in their championing of it. They believed it would be a more suitable and long-lasting name, and Knight grudgingly agreed.

Travis won the 1903 U.S. Amateur title with the Schenectady, driving its popularity even higher. His most spectacular performance with the putter would come almost a year later, when he boarded an ocean liner and sailed for Great Britain to compete in the British Amateur at Royal St. George's Golf Club at Sandwich on England's southeastern coast.

Travis's game was well prepared when he arrived at Royal St. George's. He was not prepared, however, for the cold shoulder he received from his hosts. None of the top players offered to play practice rounds with him nor offered to have a drink or a meal in the evening.

When it came to the event itself, the warmth kept coming, Royal St. George's declined to provide Travis with a locker; he had to change clothes in a small hallway, and he had to store his clubs in the pro shop each night. When it came to the assignment of a caddie, the Royal St. George's caddie master gave Travis the bottom of the barrel—a slow-witted, visually impaired man in his late twenties, whose knowledge of the game was woefully lacking. On the eve of the tournament, local bookies made the odds on Travis at 30 to 1.

Consistently outdistanced from the tee by opponents, Travis's short game more than offset this shortcoming, especially his putting with the Schenectady. On the way to the final, he took down the two biggest names in British Golf: Harold Hilton and Horace Hutchinson.

In the thirty-six-hole final, Travis faced off against the longest hitter Great Britain had to offer, Edward Blackwell, who played out of the Royal and Ancient Club of St. Andrews. Most observers, although thoroughly rattled by his short game, believed that Blackwell's far superior length off the tee would be impossible for the short-hitting Travis to overcome.

Travis came out of the gate with his Schenectady putter red-hot, winning four of the first five holes. He would take the title easily, closing out the match at the thirty-third hole.

When Travis returned home, he received quite the hero's welcome. Citing the fact that he was the U.S. Amateur and the British Amateur champion, the *New York Times* dubbed him the "World Champion of Golf." His British Amateur trophy was put on display in a high-profile location: the window of Tiffany's.

A SAND TRAP IN A DEPARTMENT STORE

Today winning the Masters brings the champion a treasure trove of endorsements and other revenue-generating circumstances. The winners of the Masters in its early years had a much more limited range of opportunities. There is no better example of this than Gene Sarazen in 1935.

Craig Wood was already in the clubhouse with a three-stroke lead over Sarazen as Sarazen teed off on the par-five fifteenth hole. The press corps covering the Masters was so sure that Wood would be the winner that they goaded Wood and his wife into posing for a photo with the winner's check.

It was at about that moment that Sarazen hit the shot that most golf enthusiasts believe is the single most famous stroke of golf ever played. Grantland Rice described it in his nationally syndicated column the next day as "the shot heard 'round the world." The shot, Sarazen's second on the par-five fifteenth, was with a four-wood from 232 yards, and it found the bottom of the cup for a double eagle.

Bobby Jones was one of the few people who witnessed the shot. He was standing on a mound about fifty yards away from Sarazen. "His swing into the ball was so perfect and so free," Jones said, "one knew immediately that it was a gorgeous shot."

With that one swing, Sarazen had wiped out a three-shot deficit. He parred his remaining three holes and defeated Wood handily the next day in a thirty-six-hole playoff.

A few weeks after his win at the Masters, Sarazen was the main attraction not on any type of national stage but in the marble and glass structure of Hecht's Department Store at the corner of Seventh and F Street in Washington DC. Hecht's was a regional chain that operated mainly in the mid-Atlantic states, and the DC store was its flagship location.

Hecht's had retained Sarazen to promote golf products to its customers, and the store constructed a sand trap for him to demonstrate bunker shots. Sarazen put on two two-hour sessions to overflow crowds. In these sessions he went over the ABCs of golf, demonstrated sand shots, and fielded questions from the audience. He also talked about his shot heard 'round the world and held up the four-wood he had used for all to see.

A BIG CHANGE FOR THE UNITED STATES OPEN

In early 1965 the United States Golf Association announced it was ending one of the long-standing traditions of the men's U.S. Open Championship. For decades the Open had been contested over three days, with thirty-six holes being played on the final day. But henceforth, the association's foremost event would be played over four days.

There had been grumblings for some time about the previous format. These concerns intensified with Ken Venturi's problems on the final day of the 1964 Open at the Congressional Country Club near Washington DC. He claimed the title but almost collapsed from heat exhaustion near the finish.

The USGA acknowledged that player well-being, highlighted by Venturi's struggle, was a consideration. But the association added there were other factors as well: slow play, which had grown worse with the adoption of the recent rules at the green that allowed players to clean their golf balls and repair ball marks; weather delay concerns; and expanded television coverage.

Not everyone was happy with the change. Among these were two-time Open champion Gene Sarazen, Chick Evans, the first Amateur player to win the Open crown, and surprisingly, Ken Venturi, who stated, "I don't think I would have won at Congressional if I had had to wait another day to go out on the course." Among those heralding the change was two-time United States Amateur champion and future commissioner of the PGA, Deane Beman. He had participated in nine U.S. Opens, and he called the change "bold and progressive."

ARNIE THE PILOT

In late February 1966 Arnold Palmer, off to his fastest start ever on the PGA Tour with a win, two seconds, and a third in his first five starts, took delivery at an airport near his Latrobe, Pennsylvania, home of an item that would make travel between tour stops faster than it had ever been before, a $750,000 airplane: the Aero Twin Jet Commander.

Arnie had taken his first flying lesson ten years earlier and was now an accomplished pilot. Two days after taking delivery of this plane, he piloted it to New York City to attend the Metropolitan Golf Writers Association's dinner and accept the group's Golden Tee Award for his career achievements.

Arnie enjoyed being in the pilot's seat almost as much as he enjoyed golf. In 1976 he was part of a three-pilot team that established a world record for an around-the-world flight. Departing Denver, Colorado, in a Learjet, the trio—making refueling stops in Boston, Paris, Tehran, Sri Lanka, Jakarta, Manila, Wake Island, and Honolulu—circled the globe in fifty-seven hours, twenty-five minutes, shattering the old record of eighty-six hours, nine minutes.

In 2010 Arnie was one of six men to receive a Wright Brothers Master Pilot Certificate from the Federal Aviation Administration for expertise and safe operations over more than fifty years. Among the other recipients were former astronauts Neil Armstrong and Gene Cernan. Arnie elected to retire from the pilot's seat in January 2011, at age eighty-one.

UNDER UNUSUAL CIRCUMSTANCES, A PLAYER MAKES QUITE A DEBUT IN A U.S. OPEN

Philip Perkins, the 1928 British Amateur champion, had relocated to the United States shortly after that victory. Three weeks before teeing it up in the 1932 United States Open at the Fresh Meadow Country Club in New York City, Perkins had turned professional. In the months preceding the event, his practice time had been limited due to the fact he was recovering from a gunshot wound.

Since relocating to the United States, Perkins had been a regular in the country's top amateur events. Several months before the U.S. Open, Perkins played in his final amateur tournament, the Dixie Amateur in Miami. Perkins had reached the finals but then had to forfeit the match after being shot in a robbery attempt.

The evening before the scheduled final, Perkins had been at one of Miami's most popular nightclubs. Shortly before midnight, six men brandishing pistols burst into the establishment, intent on robbing the club and its patrons. The robbers lined the customers and employees up against a wall. In this roundup were two plainclothes police officers, who had been enjoying a complimentary meal at the club. A few moments after they had been lined up against the wall, the officers pulled out their weapons and opened fire. Mayhem ensued. One of the robbers grabbed Perkins and used him as a human shield. When the firing stopped, one robber was dead, three were wounded and in custody, and two had escaped. Perkins was one of several patrons who had been wounded. He was shot in the thigh.

In the Open, Perkins showed no ill effects from the wound. He was on the leaderboard the first two rounds, and in the third round he vaulted into the lead.

Before the start of the final round, the word around the clubhouse was that Perkins would crack under the pressure. That would prove not to be the case—Perkins seemed to thrive on it. His only slipup in his round came at the sixteenth hole, when he recorded his lone three-putt of the tournament.

At the final hole Perkins stood over a seven-foot birdie putt that would give him an even-par 70 for the round. He addressed his ball but then abruptly backed away. He had been distracted by the winding sound of a newsreel camera. Perkins asked the cameraman if he would mind turning off his camera, and if he did, Perkins would reenact the putt for him, once he had holed out. The cameraman complied.

Perkins then confidently rolled in his putt for birdie. After a few moments of acknowledging the cheers of the gallery, he returned to the spot where he had putted from to do one for the camera. He made that one as well.

Perkins was the leader in the clubhouse, but in short order Bobby Cruickshank matched his seventy-two-hole total. It looked like there would be a playoff. Then word came that Gene Sarazen, the recent winner of the British Open, was setting the back nine on fire. He had surged into a three-stroke lead ahead of Perkins and Cruickshank by the time he reached the tee of the final hole.

As Sarazen prepared to play his approach to the final green, there was very little drama, but there would soon be plenty of chaos. By this time most of the ten thousand fans in attendance were now bunched around the eighteenth green and down both sides of the fairway. After his approach shot landed in a greenside bunker, all crowd control measures broke down. The throng surged onto the final green.

It was proving almost impossible to get the crowd under control. Gene and his playing partner struggled to make it through the throng. Security had only cleared about a quarter of the green when Gene's patience expired; he decided to go ahead and play his shot from the bunker.

Standing a few feet behind the bunker was Gene's good friend Paul Gallico, the sports editor of the *New York Daily News*. Gallico would later become a noted novelist and short story writer. His works would include the tearjerker *The Snow Goose* and *The Poseidon Adventure*. Gallico pleaded with Gene to wait for more of the green to be cleared, but Gene ignored his pleas. His blast from the sand stopped eight feet from the cup.

The crowd surged again and enveloped Gene, leaving him in a twenty-foot circle. Gene wasted no time. He calmly rolled in the putt for par and a three-stroke victory.

BASEBALL ALMOST LOSES OUT TO AUGUSTA NATIONAL

For years the only thing the hapless Washington Senators baseball franchise had going for it was the privilege of hosting the opening day of the baseball season for the American League. The reason: so the president of the United States could throw out the first ball.

President Taft started the tradition of throwing out the first ball at the Washington team's opening day in 1910. Since Taft's first throw, the president's participation in the opening day ceremonies had become a colorful part of the national pastime. Only a few times since then, because of war or other emergencies, had a president not filled this role.

In 1953, because the newly elected president, Dwight Eisenhower, had been a star baseball player in high school and was a huge fan of Major League Baseball, baseball officials and fans of the game were shocked to learn he was going to skip the throwing out the first ball tradition in favor of starting his own tradition, an Augusta National Golf Club one.

Eisenhower's new tradition was a weeklong golf vacation at Augusta National the week after the Masters, which typically included a round with the winner of that year's tournament. It was a tradition he would enjoy seven out of the eight years he was in the White House.

Opening day for the Washington team was set for the day after Eisenhower's scheduled departure for Augusta. A scheduling snafu already had Eisenhower interrupting his vacation for a quick one-day trip back to Washington DC the day after the opener to give an address to the American Newspaper Editors Association. And much to the dismay of Major League Baseball, he was not about to give up any more Augusta time. Vice President Nixon was instructed to warm up; he was going to pinch hit for Eisenhower and throw out the first ball.

Ben Hogan won the Masters the day before Eisenhower's arrival with a record-setting score of fourteen-under par. Eisenhower's goal for this trip was to set a personal record. He was seeking for the first time to break 90 at Augusta National. He didn't come close in his first two rounds, the second of which was played with Hogan.

After he concluded that round, he received word that rain had forced the postponement of the baseball game back in Washington DC. Since he was going to be in Washington on the next day anyway to deliver his speech, the American League office had contacted Eisenhower's chief of staff at the White House and asked if the president could now accommodate them and throw out the first ball. Eisenhower said yes. Before dinner that evening, he wanted to make sure his arm would be ready for his first ball duties, so he and an aide had a brief game of catch behind the Augusta National clubhouse.

The next day Eisenhower's arm was ready, but his stomach was not. After his game of catch, he dined in the Augusta National dining room and soon thereafter developed symptoms of food poisoning. Despite being in tremendous discomfort, Eisenhower gamely flew to Washington to honor his commitments.

During his speech to the American Newspaper Editors Association, he had to cling to the lectern, and several times he thought he was about to faint. After the speech, aides found a spot with a couch for Eisenhower to lie down for a few minutes before he had to leave for the ballpark.

At the game he made the throw and then ducked out of the stadium at the end of the second inning, flew back to Augusta, and spent the next two days in bed. On the third day, he was back on the course and accomplished his goal of breaking 90 with an 88. The following day, the last of his stay, he teed it up again and again broke 90, this time with an 86.

BEN WHO?

When a young man from Ohio and his fiancé had an opportunity to go to South East England for the British Open in 2003 at Royal St. George's Golf Club, they were all in. The two were anxious to soak up all of the experience. On day 2 of the tournament, a new British acquaintance was surprised to see the young man buying T-shirts in a souvenir stand at the course. The reason he was surprised was this was not something you see an individual who is near the top of the leaderboard in the British Open doing. The acquaintance was a British caddie whom the young man had hooked up with upon arriving at Royal St. George's.

The young man's name was Ben Curtis, and he was in forty-eight hours going to be one of golf's biggest ever "Cinderella stories." The term *out of nowhere* didn't seem to do him justice. He was from the bosom of Middle America, Ostrander, Ohio. He had attended Kent State University and had played on the golf team.

Ben turned professional in 2000. He toiled on the Hooters Tour, picking up one win before qualifying for the PGA Tour 2003 season with a twenty-sixth-place finish at the Q-School. Before he arrived in England for the British Open, he had played in just thirteen events and had yet to record a top-ten finish.

Ben slipped into the field with a thirteenth-place finish in the Western Open. The top eight finishers in that event who had not already qualified received invites to the British Open. Five of the top thirteen had previously qualified, which sent thirteenth finisher Ben, the No. 396-ranked player in the world, on the way to England to play in golf's oldest major.

Royal St. George's offered up quite the test. It was pure links golf: hard-baked greens, crosswinds, punishing rough, and there was seemingly nothing flat about it, producing odd bounces more bad than good. It was a course that called for patience and inner calm.

Ben was undaunted by its challenges. In the opening round he shot a 72, which put him ahead of Tiger Woods. Ben was also ahead of Phil Mickelson, Padraig Harrington, and the defending champion, Ernie Els.

In rounds 2 and 3 Ben shot 72 and 70, respectively. This placed him in a five-way tie for third place, two strokes behind the leader, Thomas Bjørn. That a player with minimal experience in top-flight golf, let alone links golf, could be in this position was quite remarkable. Ben's performance was even more impressive because he had managed it without a coach.

In the final round Ben was playing several groups ahead of Bjørn. He had an excellent front nine of three under and briefly took the lead, but in a four-hole stretch, he made three bogeys, and it appeared that his chance was gone. Two strokes behind at this point, Ben was receiving a thunderous ovation for his effort for the week as he walked up the eighteenth fairway, and he could take solace in the fact he was going to receive a healthy check.

But unbeknownst to Ben, disaster was striking Bjørn back at the par-three sixteenth. His tee shot was just a little right and caught the portion of the green that was sloped to the right, and his ball trickled into a bunker. His next shot landed on the green but did not clear the area that was sloped. It rolled back into the bunker. His next effort did the same thing. With his third shot from the sand, he made it past the slope and one-putted for a double bogey. He was now tied with Ben for the lead.

Up ahead at eighteen, Ben was long with his approach and had a lengthy chip back to the hole. His chip was too strong, leaving him a ten-footer. He calmly rolled it in for his par.

Bjørn dropped one shot behind Ben at the seventeenth, when he missed the green with his approach and could not get up and down for par. Bjørn's approach at eighteen was just short. Ben had gone to the practice range to stay loose for a playoff. Bjørn's chip for birdie to tie Ben turned away just short of the hole, and Ben Curtis was the British Open champion.

Ben joined Francis Ouimet, the winner of the 1913 U.S. Open, as the only other player to win in his first appearance in a major. Ben's first-place check was for $1,112,720.

HE SCOFFS AT A HUGE FINE BY THE GOVERNMENT, THEN COMES OFF THE COURSE TWICE TO HELP SAVE THE UNITED STATES FROM A FINANCIAL MELTDOWN

In the summer of 1907, President Theodore Roosevelt's big push to break up large trusts was making its way through the court system. One of the most noteworthy cases to be ruled upon was against John D. Rockefeller's Standard Oil empire. The ruling came in August. The federal judge in this particular case was Kenesaw Mountain Landis, who would later be hired by Major League Baseball to clean up that game, after the Black Sox Scandal in 1919.

Landis ruled that Standard Oil had accepted illegal kickbacks on shipments from a railroad company, and he imposed the largest fine in United States court history. Out for his daily round of golf, Rockefeller was about to tee off on the fifth hole when a messenger scurried out to deliver a note from Standard Oil's attorney on Landis's ruling and the size of the fine. Rockefeller read the note, calmly placed it in his pocket, and unleashed his best drive of the day.

A few minutes later, a member of his foursome mustered the courage to ask the amount of the fine. "Twenty-nine million, two hundred and forty thousand," Rockefeller replied. "The maximum penalty, I believe."

Later Rockefeller would remark, "Judge Landis will be dead a long time before this fine is paid." The fine would never be paid. The verdict and sentence were reversed by the United States Court of Appeals almost a year later.

In early October of 1907, just a few months after Landis's ruling, the country's most severe financial crisis to date began to unfold, and Rockefeller would be called upon to help quell it. Known as the Panic of 1907, this crisis would lead to the establishment of the Federal Reserve and the FDIC, the Federal Deposit Insurance Corporation. The Panic of 1907 had many elements in common with the financial crisis of 2007–9. Both crises started among New York City financial institutions and markets, and both affected the economy of the United States and the rest of the world.

The trigger for the panic was a failed scheme by speculators to corner the copper market. The failure of the scheme impacted banks and trusts in the New York City financial market. This created grave concern among customers that in only a few days turned into a stampede by them to withdraw their funds. This run on banks and trusts in New York City spread like wildfire across the country.

For the last almost quarter of a century, J. P. Morgan had been acting as the country's unofficial financial guardian and had used the vast amount of funds at his disposal to support the financial markets in periods of crisis. But this crisis had erupted so quickly and spread with such momentum that it had outstripped even Morgan's ability to contain it.

Two weeks into the crisis, banks across the country were failing in large numbers. As the crisis was fast approaching the point of no return, Morgan reached out to Rockefeller and several more of the country's most financially powerful individuals. Morgan raised what would in today's dollars amount to almost a half-billion to undergird the financial markets.

The financial contagion that had swept the country was fueled in no small part by rumors and misinformation. This was the case even in the reporting on Morgan's efforts in raising the funds to end the crisis. John D. Rockefeller had provided 40 percent of the funds Morgan gathered to stave it off. In several New York City papers the following day, it was reported that the frenzied crowds jamming the streets of the financial district had sent up a huge cheer when Rockefeller arrived at the steps of the Morgan Bank to make his pledge.

But in fact, Rockefeller never made it down to the financial district that day. He was twenty-five miles away at his estate in the Pocantico Hills playing a round of golf on his private course.

To increase the amount of exercise he obtained during a round, Rockefeller had taken to riding a bike on the course between shots. Rockefeller was informed by a messenger that J. P. Morgan was on the telephone. The nearest phone was in his barn. Rockefeller pedaled over to it to take the call. He granted Morgan's request for a pledge of funds. Rockefeller then returned to the course and resumed his round. He had played only a few more holes when he was again informed by a messenger that Morgan was again on the telephone. Rockefeller pedaled back to the barn. Morgan needed Rockefeller to increase his initial pledge, and he agreed to do so. He then pedaled back out to the course to finish his game.

According to a story in the *Washington Post*, several weeks after Rockefeller had helped stave off the banking crisis, an enterprising gentleman ventured out to Rockefeller's estate outside New York City. He pitched an investment opportunity to Rockefeller. The oil magnate was very attracted to the proposition. In an attempt to close the deal, the man dropped a big name who had already agreed to become a principal investor in the venture.

Upon hearing the man's name, Rockefeller did a one-eighty. He advised the gentleman he was no longer interested in his project. Rockefeller then proceeded to tell the gentleman why he had soured on the deal. He had recently had a dispute with the big-name investor the gentleman had just mentioned. The dispute was over a golf match the two had played on the course at Rockefeller's estate. In the match the man had expressed the opinion that Rockefeller had not played by the rules of golf.

Rockefeller and this man were evenly matched in their golf ability and about the same age. Rockefeller had extended the invitation for the match and had spent a number of days practicing earnestly for it. This man was very well-known as well, and it was agreed upon that there would be no press or spectators present for the contest; the only witnesses to the proceedings would be their caddies.

The match was to be decided by stroke play, and it was a nip and tuck contest. What triggered their dispute took place at the sixteenth hole, when Rockefeller struck a splendid shot from behind a fairway bunker to the green. He then holed out in two putts. And as Rockefeller was walking off the green, he declared that he was in the lead by one stroke. His competitor took issue with Rockefeller. He believed that Rockefeller had actually been in the fairway bunker and had illegally moved his ball out of the sand—a two-stroke penalty. Taking that into account, his competitor believed that he was in the lead by one stroke.

Both men became incensed at the other. And they played the last two holes as if they had millions riding on the outcome. But they halved those two holes. Rockefeller finished with what he thought was a score of 85 to his opponent's 86. His opponent contended that Rockefeller had scored an 87. The two jawed at each other on the quarter-mile hike from the course back to the Rockefeller mansion. And instead of staying for dinner as planned, the competitor abruptly departed and returned to his home on Fifth Avenue in the city.

Some five months after the match, the two had not communicated with each other, and each was still of the opinion that he had won by one stroke. Had they been playing for millions that day, Rockefeller's competitor would not have had any problem coming up with the funds. His name was Andrew Carnegie.

IT LOOKED LIKE AN ICE CREAM SCOOP ON A STICK

It seemed fitting that Horton Smith won the first Masters Tournament in 1934 at Bobby Jones's Augusta National Golf Club. In 1930, the year Jones won the Grand Slam, winning all four of golf's major tournaments, Jones executed perhaps the most fantastic shot in his Grand Slam run, thanks largely to Smith's generosity.

In 1928 golfers received some welcomed relief when a Texan by the name of Edwin Kerr MacClain invented and patented a club specifically designed for the sand. A member of the Houston Country Club, MacClain had a penchant for landing in bunkers. Frustrated by the fact that there was nothing more useful than a niblick (a modern-day nine-iron) for extricating his ball from the sand, MacClain took matters into his own hands and designed a club for that purpose.

The club was far from a joy to the eye. It had a strange concave face, and it resembled a large ice cream scoop on a stick. But it certainly got the job done.

In early 1930, during their play in the Southeastern Open in Augusta, Horton Smith, who had won eight times on tour the year before, gave

Bobby Jones a MacClain sand wedge. It would prove to be a very valuable addition to Jones's bag. That summer in the British Open at Hoylake, the second leg of his grand slam, Jones had a two-stroke lead in the final round when he hit a wayward approach shot on the sixteenth hole that ended up in a greenside bunker. It was a nasty lie near the bunker's greenside lip.

Jones took the MacClain sand wedge out of his bag. The lie forced him to stand with one foot in the sand and the other on a grassy slope. His blast from the sand stopped four inches from the cup, and Jones's victory was virtually assured.

The scooping action of the MacClain sand wedge met with the disfavor of the United States Golf Association and the golf governing body of Great Britain, the Royal and Ancient Club of St. Andrews, and they outlawed its use in 1931.

NIXON'S GOLF

An invite to play a round with President Eisenhower at Burning Tree was a much hoped-for request among Washington DC circles. One of those anxiously awaiting the call was his vice president, Richard Nixon.

Nixon had played football in college, but that pretty much ends the athletic comparison of the two, and even that shared experience was radically different. Eisenhower was on his way to being a star at West Point until a knee injury ended his football career. Nixon was a scrub on the Whittier College team, where he was scrimmage fodder for the first team during practice and then rode the bench on game day. He played end and had a build woefully smaller than his first-team counterparts. The Whittier coach believed his players should always go all out and not let up in practice, so Nixon took a pounding each day. But he won the respect of his teammates, for each time they mowed him down, he would get up, dust himself off, and then give it everything he had on the next play, which, unfortunately for him, wasn't much.

Nixon's golf game wasn't much either. He had taken up the game only three years earlier and had played more out of political necessity than anything else. Soon after Eisenhower's inauguration in 1953, there were press reports of Nixon being a frequent patron of a local public driving range, working on his game in anticipation of getting a call from the president. He did not have to wait too long. The call came in early May of Eisenhower's first year in office.

Eisenhower thought Nixon had to be sandbagging his reported twenty handicap and picked him as his partner. Nixon's play that day validated he was, at a bare minimum, a twenty handicapper, and he and Eisenhower took a beating. Later Nixon would write about the occasion and describe how after the round Eisenhower chewed him out like a Dutch uncle, saying, "Look here; you're young, you're strong, and you can do a lot better than that!" Shamed into taking up the game seriously, Nixon took lessons and began to play regularly. By Eisenhower's second term, he was playing to a twelve handicap.

Even with the improvement of his game, future golf games for Nixon with Eisenhower were few and far between. One happened in early October 1957, when Eisenhower was trying to overcome a bad stretch. While he was on vacation in Newport, Rhode Island, he had tried to quell the Little Rock school desegregation crisis between golf rounds at the Newport Country Club. His attempts to get a handle on the situation broke down, and he finally had to send a contingent of one thousand troops from the 101st Airborne Division to ensure the federal court's desegregation order would be carried out and that law and order would be maintained.

Eisenhower returned to Washington from Newport on October 1. Three days later he sent a message to Richard Nixon's office, asking his vice president if he thought it was safe to play golf and, if so, could he join him at Burning Tree that afternoon. Nixon answered affirmatively to both questions. It would be Eisenhower's last chance to relax before another huge event that caused the editors of *Life* magazine to warn, "The world might be at a turning point."

While Nixon and Eisenhower were playing Burning Tree that fateful day, half a world away, the Soviet Union was teeing up a ball of its own. It was about the size of a beach ball and weighed 184 pounds. It would be propelled into flight by several huge cylinders filled with a combination of liquid oxygen and kerosene. That evening the Soviets pulled off one of the biggest shots of the twentieth century, when they sent Sputnik, the Earth's first artificial satellite, into orbit, and the Space Race was on.

In January 1969, a few days after his inauguration as president, Richard Nixon happened to look down at a portion of the floor in the Oval Office. He noticed that Eisenhower had left his mark on it. It was pockmarked from his golf spikes where he had walked into and out of the office after his practice sessions on the White House's South Lawn. Nixon had that section of the floor removed and sent to the Eisenhower Library in Abilene, Kansas.

For all practical purposes, Nixon gave up golf while he was president, but he was well aware of the game's popularity with the public. He always called to congratulate the winner of the U.S. Open, and key figures in the game were frequent guests at White House functions.

The Reverend Billy Graham could confirm Nixon was also very attentive to the importance of golf to his friends. During Nixon's first term in office, Graham was traveling in France when he decided to get in a round of golf. Since he had not brought his clubs on the trip, he rented a set from the pro shop at the course he was playing. Graham proceeded to play one of the best rounds of his life with the rented clubs. After his game, he immediately went to the pro shop and tried to purchase the clubs, but the individual manning the pro shop refused to sell them. Several months later the set of clubs Graham had coveted arrived at his North Carolina home. Nixon had heard of the incident and used the Oval Office's sway to secure them for Graham.

After the Watergate scandal forced Nixon to resign, he had plenty of time on his hands and he began to play golf again, teeing it up several times a week at a course near his San Clemente, California, home. One of his aides was a talented golfer and worked with Nixon on his game, and he ultimately shot the best round of his life, a 78. As more time passed after his resignation, Nixon gradually began to become more active with other pursuits, particularly writing, and he gave up golf.

WHITE HOUSE HELICOPTER GOES OUT OF BOUNDS

In late May 1994 David Watkins, President Bill Clinton's director of the White House Office of Administration, was forced to resign from his $125,000-a-year post over the outcry he created by using a White House helicopter to transport himself and another staffer to the Holly Hill Country Club near Frederick, Maryland, for a round of golf.

Coverage of the trip, with photos of the White House helicopter and its crew of United States Marines at the country club, by a newspaper in the Frederick area created a furious outcry from the public and elected officials. Initially, there were reports that the trip was a "training mission" to familiarize Watkins with all aspects of the course, especially those aspects related to the actual time of play and associated security plans—in case President Clinton ever chose to play the course, which was located near Camp David, the presidential retreat.

A day later the White House stated that Watkins's job duties did not involve those responsibilities and that President Clinton was very upset over Watkins's actions. After a brief inquiry, a top Clinton aide directed Watkins to resign. It would later be announced that the cost of the trip, which would have taken an hour by automobile, was $13,129.

OVERRATED?

In 2015 Rickie Fowler arrived at TPC Sawgrass for the Players Championship, sharing a dubious distinction with Ian Poulter. One of the questions in the recently released *Sports Illustrated* magazine's annual player survey, in which players did not give their names, was to pick the most overrated player on the PGA Tour. Fowler and Ian Poulter shared first place.

Fowler, twenty-six, had joined the tour as a twenty-year-old rookie in 2010 with an aggressive playing style and an impressive amateur record. But before this tournament, Fowler had won only once, at the Wells Fargo Championship in 2012.

But when the tournament was finally completed in the early evening on Mother's Day Sunday, Fowler showed his peers and the rest of the world there was nothing overrated about him. The Stadium Course had provided great drama over the last three decades. Fowler's performance down the stretch tops them all. He played the final four holes making three birdies and a tap-in eagle on the par-five sixteenth hole.

While Fowler was lacking the respect of some of his peers, he was always a crowd favorite. When his birdie putt dropped at the seventy-second hole to give him the clubhouse lead, the huge gallery exploded in cheers. Fowler would have to wait over an hour to see if his score of twelve under par would hold up.

Both Sergio Garcia and Kevin Kisner were tied with Fowler when they reached the final hole. Both had makable birdie putts for the win. Garcia's putt was off line; Kisner's rimmed out. The three then had a three-hole aggregate playoff beginning at the sixteenth. The trio parred sixteen.

Fowler and Kisner birdied seventeen. Garcia had par. The trio parred eighteen, and Garcia was eliminated. The playoff now went to sudden death between Fowler and Kisner, and it started on the seventeenth.

Fowler had already birdied the daunting "Island Green" seventeenth twice that day and two more times in the other three rounds. The pin was located fifteen feet from the right edge. Kisner's shot was a little long, leaving him a twelve-footer. Fowler had saved his best tee shot at the hole for this moment. It landed softy just inside of five feet. Kisner missed his putt by two inches. Fowler drained his for the win.

As he left the seventeenth after the winning putt, his mom, Lynne, was waiting for him. They embraced, and Rickie whispered in her ear, "Happy Mother's Day."

Lynne had almost missed seeing Rickie's big moment in person. While Rickie was burning up the final holes of regulation, Lynne and Rickie's sister, Taylor, were burning down I-95. They'd had lunch with Rickie at Sawgrass. When it appeared Rickie's final round had stalled out on the front nine, Lynne and Taylor decided to head for the airport to catch a flight home to San Diego. On the way to the airport, they stopped at a dog park to give the two shih tzu dogs they were traveling with a workout.

They had already checked in and their bags were being loaded onto the plane when they received a text that Rickie had charged into the hunt. They let their checked bags head on home, and with Taylor behind the wheel of one of the tournament's courtesy cars, they made a mad dash back to Sawgrass.

Lynne and Taylor made it back in time for the start of the aggregate playoff. However, they had to watch it on a TV set in the clubhouse because they couldn't find anyone to watch the dogs. But when Rickie and Kevin Kisner remained tied after the three-hole aggregate and returned to number seventeen, arrangements were made for the dogs, and Lynne and Taylor were able to get down to the seventeenth green to see Rickie win it.

A PRESIDENT OVERDOSES ON GOLF

To succeed him as president, Teddy Roosevelt had handpicked Howard Taft, his secretary of war, to be the Republican Party's nominee in 1908. On an early campaign swing through the Midwest, Taft created quite a stir when he took a few breaks to play golf. Mail began pouring into Roosevelt at the White House, critical of the preoccupation with the game by the man he had selected to succeed him. Roosevelt fired off a letter to Taft with a dire warning about his golf playing. He wrote: "I have received literally hundreds of letters from the West protesting about it. I myself play tennis, but that game is a little more familiar; besides, you never saw a photograph of me playing tennis; photographs on horseback, yes; tennis, no. And golf is fatal."

Taft chose to ignore Roosevelt's advice and even turned up the focus on his golf. To a large gathering at a campaign stop in South Dakota, he said:

They said that I have been playing golf this summer, and that it is a rich man's game, and that it indicated I was out of sympathy with the plain people. I want to state my case before the bar of public opinion on the subject of that game of golf . . . It is a game for people who are not active enough for baseball or tennis, and yet when a man weighs 295 pounds, you have to give him some opportunity to make his legs and muscles move, and golf offers that opportunity.

Taft went on to handily defeat his Democrat opponent, William Jennings Bryan. After his election, Taft went almost immediately to Hot Springs, Virginia, to recover from the campaign and tee it up. Several weeks later he moved farther south to Augusta, where he golfed practically every day for over a month.

To clear the deck for Taft in the public's eye, Roosevelt decided to leave the country for a year to safari in Africa. This action had the reverse effect. The papers covered Roosevelt's exploits in Africa as if he were still the president of the United States. And of course, the press coverage was easy to understand because Roosevelt's activities were of more interest to the public than the activities of the current president. It seemed all Taft was doing, while Roosevelt was trekking around Africa killing lions, was trekking around golf courses in Washington DC and at vacation resorts. And the Taft stories were almost always the same. He played golf with a business tycoon or his golf score for a round was such and such or he sprained an ankle playing golf. As a result, his golf game became anathema to the press and the public as well.

By his admission Taft was not suited for the presidency, and he used golf as an escape. To make matters worse, he did not like dealing with the press. He afforded them very little access, which compounded his image problem. One of the favorite lines bantered around about Taft was "He hardly gets fairly settled down to golf before presidential duties interrupt him."

By early 1912 Theodore Roosevelt had become so disenchanted with Taft that he decided to challenge him for the Republican Party nomination for that year's presidential election. Taft managed to defeat Roosevelt's challenge at the party's convention, but Roosevelt regrouped and mounted a campaign as a third-party candidate.

It was a very tough campaign, featuring the two former allies and the Democratic nominee, Woodrow Wilson. In the closing weeks of the race, it became apparent that Taft would finish in third place. On the eve of the election, Taft returned to his hometown of Cincinnati, Ohio, to cast his vote. On Election Day he played a round of golf and then went to the polling booth to vote. Wilson won easily, taking 435 electoral votes to Roosevelt's 88 and Taft's 8.

A PRESIDENT PLAYS AN ENORMOUS AMOUNT OF GOLF WITHOUT ANY CRITICISM

No American president played more golf than Woodrow Wilson, and he did it without receiving any negative press, adverse public reaction, or political sniping.

Wilson began playing golf in 1895 while he was a professor at Princeton University, but his interest in the game was lukewarm at best. After he became president of Princeton in 1902, a trustee, mining magnate Cleveland H. Dodge, a member of long standing of the St. Andrew's Golf Club in Yonkers, thought a man in Wilson's position needed a first-rate set of clubs. So he had a set made for him while on a trip to Scotland. Dodge had a little trouble at customs when he returned. The customs inspector was unfamiliar with the game of golf and unsure how to record them. Tucker tried to demonstrate how they were used, but the inspector interrupted him, saying, "I'll just put them down as agriculture implements." The new clubs, however, did little to spark increased interest for Wilson.

Having suffered from digestive and stress problems for years, Wilson was far from a picture of health when he stepped into the Oval Office. Dr. Cary Grayson, the White House physician, quickly realized that Wilson would have to make some drastic changes if he was going to withstand the demands of the presidency.

Dr. Grayson immediately put Wilson on a healthier diet and an exercise regimen that was almost entirely golf based. Grayson had Wilson playing golf five and six times a week. Wilson's typical weekday would be to get up at six in the morning. After a hearty breakfast, he would head for the course with Dr. Grayson, and the two would typically play twelve holes and then return to the White House. Wilson would then freshen up and usually be at his desk in the Oval Office by midmorning. On Saturdays, Wilson and Grayson typically would play a full eighteen holes.

The more Wilson golfed, the more he enjoyed it. But it was painful to watch for his Secret Service detail and his caddie as Wilson's play was atrocious. The cornerstone of his game was a horrific slice. Wilson attributed his poor swing fundamentals to his right eye. He had suffered a retinal hemorrhage in that eye years earlier that restricted his view of the ball during his swing. He once explained his golfing plight with the eye this way: "My right eye is like a horse's. I can see straight out with it, but not sideways. As a result, I cannot take a full swing because my nose gets in the way and cuts off my view of the ball."

Many in Washington's inner circles were itching to play a round with Wilson. But he did not like to mix business with his relaxation, and he knew if he invited congressmen or senators to join him, they would invariably want to talk shop. So typically, the only person that joined him on the course was Dr. Grayson, and his game was just as bad as Wilson's.

Wilson usually displayed the proper presidential bearing, but on occasion he could be a bit of a klutz. Once he was so engrossed in a conversation that he almost stepped into the path of a streetcar on Pennsylvania Avenue. On a summer vacation in Cornish, New Hampshire, he went for a hike in the woods and became lost. When one of the newer weapons of warfare, the tank, was brought to the White House for a demonstration, Wilson, at the urging of aides, hopped in for a short ride down the White House driveway. As he was climbing out, he mistakenly grabbed a red-hot pipe that severely burned his right hand. His hand was bandaged and useless for several weeks. But the injury did not keep Wilson from the course. He continued to play, using just his left arm.

With Wilson golfing almost daily, several noteworthy events of his presidency occurred around the game. There are varying accounts about how he received the word about the sinking of the *Lusitania* by a German U-boat, one of the events that propelled the United States into World War I. One account has him learning of it before departing for the course that day. Another has him receiving word of the sinking during his round. And still another has him being given the word immediately upon his return from the course.

Presidents have to put out an enormous number of figurative fires. In December 1915 Wilson assisted in putting out an actual one after a round during a vacation in Pass Christian, Mississippi. As his car was returning from the golf course, Wilson spied flames coming from the roof of a house and yelled for his car to head to the home. Wilson darted up to the house's door, followed by his security detail, with fire extinguishers in hand that they had unstrapped from their vehicles.

The home belonged to a prominent judge. His wife, who was unaware of the situation, answered the banging on the door and was told by the president of the United States that her home was on fire. Wilson told her to show his men the way to the attic. By the time the local fire department arrived, Wilson's men had the blaze all but out.

Wilson's first wife, Ellen, died in the second year of his first term. Nine months later he bumped into Mrs. Edith Bolling Galt, the widow of a Washington DC jeweler, as he was entering the White House after a round of golf. Wilson was smitten immediately. They were married nine months later.

In 1916 Wilson ran for a second term. Supreme Court justice Charles Evans Hughes was his Republican opponent. On election night Hughes took an early lead in the eastern and midwestern states and held on through the evening. Wilson went to bed believing he had lost. He was playing golf with Dr. Grayson the next morning when he received the surprising word about California, a state that was expected to go for Hughes. Wilson had squeaked out a victory in the Golden State by 3,800 votes out of nearly a million cast. With California's 13 electoral votes in his column, Wilson was the winner, with 277 electoral votes to Hughes's 253.

A GOLF GAME ENDS A BITTER HOLLYWOOD FEUD

When twenty-year-old Howard Hughes arrived in Hollywood, California, in 1924, he had three goals: being the most famous producer of motion pictures, being the world's best golfer, and being the world's best pilot. Hughes golfed almost every day, and he went headfirst into the movie business. His first production was a comedy titled *Swell Hogan* that bombed. His next two efforts were financial successes.

His fourth film would be the most ambitious action film ever made to that point in the motion picture industry: *Hell's Angels*. It was the story of two British pilots in World War I and featured spectacular air combat scenes. Hughes would not only produce it, he would also direct it and take part in the flying scenes as one of the seventy pilots who were used in the film.

During the filming of *Swell Hogan*, Hughes took flight lessons and became a pilot. He had found his flight instructor during his daily morning golf game, as he had on several occasions observed a small plane flying over the course and performing stunts. Impressed by the pilot's ability, Hughes wrote down the plane's tail number. He tracked down the pilot and hired him as his flight instructor.

In one of the flight sequences Hughes wanted in *Hell's Angels*, the other pilots balked at his plan because it was too dangerous. Hughes climbed into the cockpit and piloted the plane himself for the sequence. The pilots were right. Hughes crashed the plane. Luckily, he walked away from the wreckage with only minor injuries, and he had gotten the film footage he wanted.

Production of *Hell's Angels* had started in late October 1927. It proved to be a lengthy and difficult undertaking. At the eighteen-month mark, which was considered about the halfway point, Hughes felt compelled to make a major and time-consuming change.

Three weeks before the filming of *Hell's Angels* began, there was a groundbreaking development in the movie industry. *The Jazz Singer*, starring Al Jolson, the first feature-length motion picture with sound, had debuted. Now, a year and a half later, talkies were fast becoming the norm, so Hughes made the call to convert *Hell's Angels* from a silent film to sound.

The transition to sound resulted in Greta Nissen, the female lead, having to be replaced because of her heavy Norwegian accent. Her replacement was an eighteen-year-old unknown blonde bombshell by the name of Jean Harlow. Before her untimely death eight years later, she would become one of Hollywood's all-time sex symbols.

Production on *Hell's Angels* dragged on, and Hughes soon was facing some stiff competition. First National Studios was going into production with a similar World War I aviation story. The title of the film was *Dawn Patrol*, and it was going to be directed by a man with a background strikingly similar to that of Hughes: Howard Hawks. He was the son of a wealthy industrialist—and a golfer—and he had a keen interest in aviation. In 1916, when he was twenty-one, Hawks had journeyed to Hollywood to make his mark in film. His quest was interrupted by World War I, during which he served in the army as a flight instructor.

Hawks's entire tour of duty was stateside, and he returned to Hollywood soon after the war ended. By the time production of *Dawn Patrol* began in February 1930, Hawks had made quite a name for himself as a director. Hughes instituted a dogfight of sorts against *Dawn Patrol*. He began buying up rights to available World War I–era aircraft to keep them out of First National's hands. He also bribed a secretary at First National and obtained a copy of the *Dawn Patrol* script. Hughes then took First National to court, claiming copyright infringement. He lost the action.

While the litigation was working its way through the court system, Hawks and First National had rushed *Dawn Patrol* through production. It opened to much acclaim, just five months after filming began. Its total cost had been just a tick over $700,000, and it would gross $1.6 million.

Hell's Angels finally got to the screen four months after *Dawn Patrol* opened. It also received much acclaim. Its total cost of production had been $2.8 million. It would earn $2.5 million at the box office.

At some point between the opening of the two films, Hughes sought to bury the hatchet with Hawks. He had bought the film rights to the book *Scarface*, the story of the rise and fall of a Chicago gangster that was based in large part on the life of Al Capone. Hughes wanted to bring it to the screen, and he wanted Hawks to direct it.

They were both members at the Lakeside Golf Club, and Hughes asked the pro to arrange a round of golf with Hawks. Hawks rebuffed the request, referring to Hughes as a son of a bitch. Hughes made a follow-up request through the pro at Lakeside, and Hawks decided to accept. The two had what has been described as a highly competitive round of golf, during which Hughes offered the directorship of *Scarface* to Hawks. After a few moments to overcome the shock caused by his recent adversary's offer, Hawks accepted.

Their collaboration resulted in one of the most controversial films ever produced. It was Hawks's first great directorial effort and would remain his favorite film throughout his long career. *Scarface*'s gritty depiction of violence was groundbreaking. Hawks balanced the violence with comedy in a style that has often been imitated by other directors. *Scarface* should have been the first great talkie gangster flick, but an extensive and lengthy battle with censors held up its release, allowing the films *Little Caesar* and *The Public Enemy* to jointly be the groundbreakers in the genre.

THE STATE OF THE UNION

The State of the Union address is an annual message delivered by the president of the United States to a joint session of Congress. The address fulfills the requirement in the Constitution for the president to periodically "give to the Congress Information of the State of the Union." It generally includes reports on the nation's budget, economy, defense, achievements, and the president's priorities and legislative proposals.

In the last seven days of 1954 and the first two days of 1955, President Eisenhower vacationed at the Augusta National Golf Club. He got in plenty of golf, and he spent a good deal of his time working on his annual State of the Union address in an office he used above the club's pro shop.

On January 6 Eisenhower delivered the address to Congress and a nationwide television audience at 12:30 p.m. The address was a long one, with a word count of 7,250 words, and it took fifty-three minutes to deliver.

After he concluded his remarks on the condition and needs of the country, President Eisenhower quickly made his way out of the Capitol

Building with his wife, Mamie, to his waiting limousine, and his motorcade sped away to the White House. There only Mamie exited the limo. It then sped away to the Burning Tree Club in nearby Bethesda, Maryland, where, despite the fact there was a light rain falling, Eisenhower played a quick nine holes before dark.

DETROIT LOSES ITS GOLF SOUL

In 2018 Palmer Park Golf Course, a municipal course that was a former mecca for Black golfers in Detroit, was closed by the city due to declining play and increased operating costs.

The course had gained fame in the 1930s and 1940s as the golfing home of boxing great Joe Louis. It reached its heyday in the 1960s, when Motown stars Smokey Robinson,

Marvin Gaye, and the Four Tops joined the legion of regulars at the course. Hard on the heels of the recording stars came two stars from the National Football League's Detroit Lions, Lem Barney and Mel Farr.

The course, a par sixty-nine, measured just over 5,700 yards and featured small greens. It was home to an assortment of top-notch hustlers who could clean out your wallet. Legend has it that one of these hustlers took enough money from Joe Louis to build a new house.

Golfers at Palmer Park Golf Course developed their own vocabulary, a string of expressions that enriched the game's lexicon. Rather than "Tee the ball up," golfers at Palmer Park said, "Stick it in the ground." A good putter was called an "undertaker" because he could "bury" the ball. Shanked shots were called "pitchouts," and short drives were "bunts."

The course featured a daily tournament called "The Train," in which participants would put down ten dollars. It was a very stiff competition that usually totaled twenty players, with the winner getting all of the pot. Of course, there were other ways to cash in, as there were plenty of side bets.

It is likely that many competing in The Train did not know the given name of the others in the field. Nicknames were the rule: "Wash Rack," "Sugar Jim," "Rifleman," "Pensacola," "Prime Minister," and "Georgia Red" are just a sample.

The person who ran the course for many years was a woman. Her name was Vernell Dykes. She was the cashier, ranger, starter, and general information center. She kept order using a microphone and her calm demeanor.

When the Buick Open was played in the area, two Black trailblazers who had competed in the event found their way to Palmer Park when it was over. Pete Hampton was the first Black player to win a PGA event, and Charlie Sifford was the first Black player to hold a PGA Tour card. Palmer Park regulars were very impressed with Hampton, as he was the longest hitter of a golf ball they had ever seen. They were also enthralled with the stories that Sifford told them about life on the PGA Tour. Over the rounds Sifford played on the course, he came up empty-handed, not taking any money from the Palmer crowd. But Sifford would leave Palmer Park with something he had not arrived with—a solid chipping game.

Before his arrival, Sifford's chipping game had gone sour, but during his days at Palmer, he was able to get it back into solid form. His next PGA event was the Hartford Open, which he won. It was his first of two wins on tour. His second would come two years later at the Los Angeles Open.

THE COUNTRY CLUB AT BROOKLINE COULD HAVE MISSED OUT

There had always been much discussion on when American golf came of age. The United States Golf Association put the matter to rest when it celebrated its one hundredth birthday in 1994. The USGA's centennial logo was derived from a well-known photograph from the 1913 United States Open.

The photo was of Francis Ouimet and his ten-year-old caddie, Eddie Lowery. The two were on a fairway at the Country Club in Brookline, Massachusetts, during the twenty-year-old Ouimet's incredible victory in the 1913 United States Open. Ouimet won the title in a playoff over two of the greatest players of that era, Great Britain's Harry Vardon and Ted Ray.

Because Vardon and Ray were coming to the United States for a tour and would be in the field at Brookline, the 1913 United States Open became the most anticipated golf event in the country's history to date. But the Country Club in Brookline could have lost out on hosting the event. The USGA had awarded the Open to the club in mid-January, just a few weeks before the announcement that Vardon and Ray would be coming to America. The dates for the event were June 3 and 4, some eight weeks before the expected arrival of Vardon and Ray.

The USGA contacted the Country Club, seeking a change in the date of the Open to mid-August to allow Vardon and Ray to be in the field. The Country Club did not agree to the change. Its managers did not believe the course would be in condition to host the event in the dead of summer. They countered with a mid-September date. Vardon and Ray were contacted, and they balked at that date.

Charles B. Macdonald then entered the discussion—the same Charles B. Macdonald who had built the first eighteen-hole course in the United States in Chicago and had won the first U.S. Amateur in 1895. Macdonald had given up his career as a stockbroker and had moved from Chicago to New York City and was now a full-time golf course architect.

Macdonald was promoting a course he had designed five years earlier, the National Golf Links on the South Fork of Long Island, as a replacement for the Country Club at Brookline. In advocating the National Golf Links for the Open, Macdonald was championing the fact that the course had just completed the installation of an irrigation system that would allow its fairways and greens to be in top condition even in mid-August.

The USGA began the process of polling the fifty-two delegates nationwide who had taken part in the selection of the Country Club and the June dates, asking for a revote that would pit the Country Club and the September dates against the National Golf Links and the mid-August dates. But before this process could be completed, the problem was unexpectedly resolved as word came from Vardon and Ray that they had reconsidered and would be available to play at Brookline in September.

THE NATION'S TOP SPORTS JOURNALIST ATTEMPTS TO QUALIFY FOR THE U.S. OPEN

The most focus to date for a golf event in the United States was on the 1920 U.S. Open at the Inverness Club in Toledo, Ohio. The reason: Great Britain golfing greats Harry Vardon and Ted Ray were back, hoping to avenge their 1913 defeat by Francis Ouimet at Brookline, and there was a long list of notable American veterans in the event's field. Also, there was a group of highly touted U.S. Open rookies who in today's parlance would carry "the young guns tag." In this group were Bobby Jones, Gene Sarazen, and Johnny Farrell. Each of these players would be future U.S. Open champions. Jones would claim the title four times, Sarazen twice, and Farrell once.

Inverness opened as a run-of-the-mill nine-hole course in 1903. In 1916 its members decided to upgrade. They brought in stellar golf course designer Donald Ross, and he reworked the course into an eighteen-hole masterpiece that created quite a buzz. It hosted the Ohio Open in 1919, and the success of that event spurred a push for the course to host the country's Open championship. The push developed into an avalanche. By the time USGA officials met to hold the vote to select the site, all the other contenders had decided to drop out.

Two hundred forty-four golfers attempted to qualify. The qualifying rounds were held at Inverness a few days before the Open. Those qualifying would play thirty-six holes on Thursday and Friday for the championship. In that large number attempting to qualify was a man who was in Toledo on business. His job was to cover the tournament for his newspaper, the *New York Herald Tribune*. His name was Grantland Rice.

Rice in 1910 had penned the lines: "For when the Great Scorer comes to mark against your name. He writes—not that you won or lost—but how you played the game." Another of his more famous writings was his description of the Notre Dame football team's backfield in 1925: "Outlined against a blue-gray October sky the Four Horsemen rode again. In dramatic lore, they are known as famine, pestilence, destruction, and death. These are only aliases. Their real names are Stuhldreher, Miller, Crowley, and Layden."

Rice had been playing golf for ten years. He had taken up the game after covering the Southern Open while he was working as the sports editor for the *Nashville Tennessean*. Rice had played football and baseball at Vanderbilt College in Nashville. He picked up his new game with relative ease with a swing that was described as fluid and seamless. His tee shots were in the 250- to 260-yard range, which with the clubs and balls of the day was considered quite a poke.

In 1911, a year after taking up golf, Rice accepted a job as a sportswriter for the *Evening Mail* in New York City. Since it was an afternoon paper, Rice's copy was in shortly after lunch, and he spent many afternoons golfing at the Englewood Golf Club just across the river in New Jersey. His length off the tee and his frequency of play soon had Rice's game at the scratch level.

Where he had plenty of free time for golf, he devoted little of his workday to covering the sport. His boss, assistant sports editor Francis Albertani, believed only stories about baseball, football, and boxing belonged on the sports page. Rice's requests to cover the 1913 U.S. Open at Brookline and the 1914 Open in Chicago were denied by Albertani.

In early 1915 Rice moved to the *New York Herald Tribune* for twice as much money as he was making at the *Evening Mail*, and his career took off. The well-heeled readers of the *Tribune* were getting into golf in a big way, and Rice was giving its readers ample material on the subject by devoting a weekly column to it. Shortly after arriving at the *Tribune*, Rice coauthored with U.S. Amateur champion Jerome Travers one of America's first books on golf, titled *The Winning Shot*.

Rice's hopes of making the field at Inverness were dashed on the first day of qualifying when he shot an 88.

THE MOST POLITICALLY SIGNIFICANT ROUND OF GOLF EVER PLAYED

What the *New York Times* called "the most politically significant round of golf ever played" took place on February 19, 1956. It happened not at one of the game's strongholds of power and influence, like Burning Tree outside Washington DC, Winged Foot near New York City, or Augusta National, but deep in southern Georgia at the Glen Arven Country Club in Thomasville.

Its importance took hold not at the first tee but at the tenth, when a sixty-five-year-old golf fanatic, who happened to be the president of the United States, stuck a tee in the ground. The previous fall Dwight Eisenhower was wrapping up his third year in the Oval Office. A recent Gallup Poll showed that 70 percent of respondents approved of the way he was handling his job. At this point his reelection to a second term was considered a lock. But that changed on September 24, 1955.

Eisenhower was in Denver, Colorado, on an extended vacation. Several hours after playing twenty-seven holes of golf at the Cherry Hills Golf Club, he suffered a heart attack. In the mid-1950s the outlook for heart attack victims was a gloomy one. The prospect of a second term for

President Eisenhower appeared to be well off the table, and a host of possible candidates from both parties began testing the waters for a run at the White House.

Eisenhower was hospitalized in Denver for six weeks. He spent a few days in Washington and then went to his farm in Gettysburg for further recuperation for most of the remainder of the year. The Professional Golfers' Association stepped in to aid in his recovery by having a practice putting green installed just a few paces from his side porch at Gettysburg. While at Gettysburg, Eisenhower found another use for his putter. He used it as a cane.

During this recuperative period, Eisenhower became convinced he was not ready for the proverbial rocking chair. His outlook was also buoyed by the recovery of another heart attack victim, a man who was a leader of the opposition party: Democratic senator Lyndon Johnson. He had suffered a heart attack three months before Eisenhower's and was running people over on the comeback trail, and he would soon be returning to his majority leader position in the Senate.

As Eisenhower's spirit and health began to improve, his focus turned toward seeking reelection. With each passing day, his personal and political future began looking stronger and stronger.

The first week in January, Eisenhower went to Key West for a week. While there, he mulled over his future and worked on his golf game, practicing pitch shots daily at a baseball field. He held a press conference on the last day of the trip, and many in the press corps remarked he had never looked or sounded better. Shortly after returning to Washington, Eisenhower held a meeting with his most trusted advisors on whether he should seek a second term. The consensus was that he should. There was one major hurdle, however, that had to be cleared before the final decision could be made. It was the report on his physical condition, to be presented at a press conference in mid-February by his medical team.

Noted heart specialist Dr. Paul Dudley White had been heading up Eisenhower's care since the day after his heart attack and would render the report. His involvement in the treatment of Eisenhower after the attack had boosted his reputation even higher, but he was looked upon by his famous patient as a bit of a loose cannon. Publicly, White was indicating that Eisenhower was in the condition to seek a second term, but privately he was trying to dissuade him.

The press conference during which White was to issue the final report was still a matter of much concern because not only would what White said have tremendous weight but also the way he said it would be equally important. White's performance when issuing the report was the high-caliber and confidence-building type Eisenhower needed, and it cleared the way for him to seek a second term.

White was quizzed at the press conference about when Eisenhower might return to the golf course. White said the consensus was he would gradually begin to play a few holes at a time. In approximately six weeks, it was expected he would be capable of playing a full eighteen holes.

After the medical team's report, Eisenhower left for a vacation at the plantation of his secretary of labor, George Humphrey, near Thomasville, Georgia. Two days after arriving, he showed up at the Glen Arven Country Club in Thomasville and played his first golf since his heart attack. He played nine holes in a steady drizzle.

A photo of Eisenhower on the first tee was on the front page of almost every paper in the country the next day. Five days later, that "most politically significant round of golf ever played" took place when Eisenhower returned to Glen Arven to play what was scheduled to be another nine-hole round. To everyone's surprise, he kept going at the turn and played a full eighteen holes. To all the press corps, he looked and acted like the old Eisenhower. He could be heard setting the wagers on the first tee and giving his opponents some needling.

Spectators and the press were allowed only to observe the first and the last hole on each side. On the eighteenth hole, a par three, he hit a poor tee shot and still had a wedge to the green for his second shot. The gathering of locals and press at the green cheered when he pitched his ball to within a few feet of the hole. Unfortunately for him, his putting was rusty, and when he missed the short putt for his par, the gathering groaned like he had just lost the U.S. Open.

Eisenhower's personal physician, Howard Snyder, accompanied him during the round. He was quizzed by reporters afterward on whether Eisenhower was not pushing it a bit by playing eighteen holes almost a month sooner than expected. Snyder replied, "All he needs is a good game—that will keep him healthy and well." He then pointed to Eisenhower's pitch shot at the last hole and said, "That will keep him happy for a long time."

In August, Eisenhower flew to the Republican National Convention in San Francisco to accept the party's presidential nomination. After his acceptance speech, he was driven from San Francisco to Monterey, California, for four days of golf at Cypress Point, playing a full eighteen holes each day.

In the November election, Eisenhower faced off against the same Democratic opponent he had handily defeated in 1952, Adlai Stevenson. It was no contest. Eisenhower won by a huge margin. His Electoral College vote count was 457 to Stevenson's 73.

GENE SARAZEN, HOWARD HUGHES, AND THE SAND WEDGE

In 1973, at age seventy-one, Gene Sarazen, winner of the 1932 British Open, was invited to play in the event that year at Royal Troon, and he accepted. Whereas Gene's ultra-famous double eagle in the 1935 Masters had been witnessed by only a handful of people, he would make a shot at Royal Troon that would be viewed by millions and millions around the world, thanks to television.

The eighth hole at Royal Troon is called the "Postage Stamp." It measures 123 yards in length and is the shortest par three in championship golf, but it rivals the twelfth at Augusta in its dastardliness. Willie Park Jr., winner of the Open in 1889, is responsible for the name; writing for a golf magazine, he described the green in a 1909 article as "a pitching surface skimmed down to the size of a postage stamp," and the name stuck. Its minuscule putting surface is difficult to hold, and anything less than a well-executed shot can run off the green and end up in one of the five deep bunkers that surround it.

The Postage Stamp has wreaked havoc on many of the biggest names in golf. In 1923 Walter Hagen made a double bogey there in the final round and finished second to Arthur Havers by one shot. In 1989 Greg Norman set a new course record of 64. His only bogey of the round came at the Postage Stamp. Tiger Woods, in contention in 1997 after a 64 in the third round, took a six on Sunday and disappeared from the leaderboard.

At the Postage Stamp in his first round in 1973, Gene teed up his ball and took a three-quarter swing with a five-iron. His ball sailed high into the air as if he had used a more lofted club. The ball landed ten feet from the flag, took two bounces, and then trickled up to the front of the cup and disappeared.

Cameras were rolling when Gene hit the shot, and in twenty-four hours it had been viewed around the world. One of the people who watched the shot on television was an old friend of Gene's whom he had not seen in some forty years.

After Gene won the U.S. Open in 1922, he spent the ensuing winter in the Los Angeles area. His days were full, playing in exhibition matches. His nights were busy as well. He played the area's nightlife circuit from the tips. He frequented the scene at the Coconut Grove nightclub at the Ambassador Hotel often, and he became a carousing pal of another young man who was hitting LA and Hollywood in a big way: Howard Hughes. The two would remain tight over the next dozen or so years.

Before Gene teed off for his second round the following day, he received a telegram from Hughes. After being seriously injured in a plane crash in 1946, Hughes, one of the world's richest men, began retreating from the public eye. By the early 1960s he was as close as you could get to total seclusion. For much of that decade, he conducted all of his business while shuttered up on the top floor of the Desert Inn Hotel in Las Vegas, Nevada. Very few people ever laid eyes on him.

Late in 1971 Hughes slipped out of Las Vegas, and he and his entourage were now holed up on an entire floor of a hotel near Buckingham Palace in London. The press had the hotel staked out, hoping to get a photo or just a snippet of information about Hughes's activities. His telegram to Gene at least gave them something. They now knew that Hughes, who in his twenties had aspired to be a championship golfer, still followed the game and that he watched television. His telegram to Gene read:

YOU HAVE NOT CHANGED A BIT. YOU ARE AS GOOD AS EVER. YOUR ACCOMPLISHMENT TODAY REFRESHED MANY PLEASANT MEMORIES.

Howard Hughes

On day 2 of the Open championship, Gene had a much larger gallery following his play than he had the day before. As one would expect, there was quite a bit of interest about what he might do for an encore at the Postage Stamp. But his tee shot there was offline and ended up in a sand trap by the green. Those who stuck around to see him play his bunker shot were well rewarded. Gene holed the shot from the bunker for a birdie two.

Although his second-round 81 matched with his opening 79 wasn't good enough to be around for the weekend, playing the Postage Stamp at three under par without ever using his putter was quite the performance for a golfer of any age. Gene holing out from a bunker was a fitting way for him to close out his British Open career. Before the 1932 tournament season, Gene's bunker play was barely average, but thanks to an assist from Howard Hughes, he would come up with the idea for the modern sand wedge.

Gene climbed into a plane piloted by Hughes for a pleasure flight. During the flight he became intrigued by the action of the flaps on a plane during takeoff, and he began to ponder the prospects of designing a club that would use the same principle to lift a ball out of a sand trap. Soon after, Gene went to work on his idea while he was spending the winter in South Florida. He reached out to his equipment company, Wilson, and had them send a half-dozen niblicks (the equivalent of a nine-iron) to him. Once the clubs arrived, he went to a local machine shop and began adjusting the angle and soldering extra lead to their sole. After long hours in the machine shop, he eventually came up with what he wanted.

Gene was staying in a rented bungalow on a nine-hole course in Port Richey. The course was far from first-rate. It had only one decent sand trap. It happened to be just a few paces from the back door of Gene's bungalow, and it became his test lab. His idea soon became a very functioning reality.

That summer Gene departed for the 1932 British Open at Prince's Golf Club at Sandwich with one of his newly created sand wedges in his bag. Given the history of Great Britain's governing golf body's reluctance to embrace American ingenuity in club design, Gene decided that at the British Open he would keep his sand wedge under wraps as much as possible and would instruct his caddie to keep the club blade down in his bag.

In the tournament Gene was able to get up and down several times from greenside bunkers with his new sand wedge. The other facets of his game were rock-solid as well. He won in a runaway with a five-stroke margin of victory. His winning total of 283 was a British Open record, besting the mark set by Bobby Jones in 1926 at St. Andrews by two strokes.

BRYSON HAD THE DISTANCE TWICE

The par-five sixth hole at Arnold Palmer's Bay Hill Golf Club and Lodge near Orlando, Florida, site of the Arnold Palmer Invitational, measures over 550 yards, and the fairway is a double bender that wraps left around a lake. Over the years the significant increases in the driving distances by players were making it within the realm of possibility that a long hitter could someday attempt to skip the fairway route and take his tee shot directly over the lake at the green some 350 yards away.

Someday came in 2003, when John Daly attempted this shot. The super-long-hitting tee shot by Daly did not make it. He tried five more times, and his ball came up short in the lake each time. He abandoned that route at that point. He walked off the green with a score of 18. At the next hole, the par-three seventeenth, he made birdie.

Eighteen years later, in 2021, after a practice round, Bryson DeChambeau, who had succeeded Daly as the PGA Tour's longest driver, let it be known that if wind conditions were right during the tournament, he would attempt to go over the water with his tee shot at the sixth.

Wind conditions were not favorable during Thursday's and Friday's rounds, but on Saturday they were. In the thick of the battle for the event's title, DeChambeau wasted no time at the tee in deciding to take on the lake. When the huge crowd at the tee box saw DeChambeau line up his tee shot to go over the water, they let out a thunderous roar.

DeChambeau took a couple of deep breaths and let it rip. A split second later, he raised his arms in celebration as he could tell that when the ball had not yet reached the halfway point of its journey, it had more than enough carry to clear the water. It landed well into the fairway and rolled into the rough on its right side, twenty yards from the green. DeChambeau pitched on and two-putted for birdie.

In the final round on Sunday, DeChambeau was tied for the lead, and again, much to the crowd's delight, he lined up his tee shot to go over the water. This time after DeChambeau struck his ball, there was no near-instant celebration on his part. Instead, a notable expression of angst covered his face. This ball was on a direct line to the green, but it was traveling on a low flight path. Its making it over the water was very much in doubt.

After several anxious moments, a huge roar went up as DeChambeau's ball cleared the lake by just a few yards and bounded into a greenside bunker. DeChambeau blasted out of the bunker. He missed his eagle putt and tapped in for birdie. Later, at the eighteenth hole, he rolled in a five-foot birdie putt to win the tournament by one stroke.

A FORMER CHAMPION TRIES TO AVOID THE HEAT BUT ENDS UP BEING TOAST

The 1912 U.S. Amateur took place in Wheaton, Illinois, at the Chicago Golf Club. It was a highly anticipated event. Harold Hilton, the top amateur in Great Britain, was the defending champion. He had sailed over to defend his title, and he was the heavy favorite. But he was dealt an embarrassing knockout blow in his first match. Hilton attributed his poor showing to the brutal heat wave that the Chicago area was experiencing during the championship.

Oppressive heat in the tournament was a factor Hilton thought he had taken off the table. Ironically, it wouldn't have been had he not sought a change in the tournament's date. The U.S. Amateur that year had been originally scheduled for early July. But when Hilton received word of the date, he requested it be rescheduled for early September, as he was given to understand that the heat in Chicago in July could be grueling. The USGA, very anxious to have Hilton in the field, agreed to his request and changed the date to the first week in September.

It turned out Hilton would have been better off playing in July, as Chicago experienced a stretch of very unseasonably low temperatures during the week the championship had been originally scheduled. That was not the case in early September, as the temperatures were unusually sweltering. In his opening match, the forty-three-year-old Hilton's game melted away in the blazing heat. And he fell to Charles Waldo Jr., a Yale College student—two down with one to go. Hilton had posted the lowest score in the thirty-six-hole qualifier the previous day. But at the scorer's table after his loss to Waldo, he said: "The heat was too much for me . . . One day I could stand, but not two."

Norman Hunter, a top-ranked young amateur from Scotland, had traveled over with Hilton for the tournament. Hunter, who for a while had held the course record at the Old Course at St. Andrews, qualified easily and won his first two matches, but he fell victim to the heat on the third day. At the midway point of this third match, he called for a doctor. The doctor examined Hunter and advised him to discontinue play. A second doctor arrived on the scene and rendered the same opinion, and Hunter conceded his match. He was put to bed for the next twenty-four hours with ice packs about his head.

Jerome Travers of New Jersey won the championship. It was his third U.S. Amateur title. His previous wins were in 1907 and 1908.

WALTER HAGEN MAKES A GROUNDBREAKING DECISION

In the fall of 1916, two leaders of the Detroit area business community, Norval Hawkins, the first sales manager for Henry Ford's automobile company, and Joseph Mack, an adman whose chief client was the Ford Motor Company, spearheaded a campaign to build a top-flight golf course in the Detroit area. They purchased 400 acres of rich farmland 25 miles outside of the city, in Bloomfield Hills, for what would become the Oakland Hills Country Club.

Hawkins and Mack brought in Donald Ross from Pinehurst, the hottest name in golf course architecture, to design the course. Ross was impressed with their site selection, declaring, "The Lord intended this for a golf links." When Ross's efforts were concluded, he had created a golfing masterpiece that has hosted the men's United States Open Championship six times.

To go with their great site and great design, Hawkins and Mack brought in a highly touted young man named Walter Hagen to be the club's golf professional. Initially, Hagen's base of operation at Oakland Hills was an old chicken coop. From this humble circumstance, he would light the fuse that would forever change the world of the professional golfer.

Hagen was an alumnus of the caddie shack. A native of Rochester, New York, and the son of a blacksmith, Hagen lived a half-mile from the Country Club of Rochester. At the age of ten, he began caddying at the club, earning a dime a round with an occasional nickel tip.

A natural athlete, Hagen picked up the game by studying the play of the club's two professionals. At age twelve he dropped out of school and spent most of his time at the club, caddying, practicing, and playing whenever he could. But his education continued in a nontraditional way. While he caddied, he studied the mannerisms, speech, and bearing of the club's members. During the winter months, he worked an assortment of part-time jobs: piano finisher, taxidermist, and mechanic. In due time at the club, he advanced to the position of assistant pro.

In early 1913 the head pro at the club departed, and Hagen moved up into the position. His responsibilities also included teaching ice skating and tennis. Later that year Hagen requested from the powers that be at the club that he be granted four days off to compete in the U.S. Open at Brookline. His request was grudgingly granted. Hagen played impressively at Brookline, finishing in fourth place, three strokes out of a playoff for the championship with Francis Ouimet, Harry Vardon, and Ted Ray.

At Brookline another participant in the field, Tom Anderson Jr., made a tremendous impression on Hagen. Anderson came from a long line of golfing professionals in Scotland, but it wasn't his game that impressed Hagen. It was his attire. Anderson wore silk shirts, colorful bandannas, and white shoes. In short order Hagen began to build his reputation for flamboyant dress on the course.

In 1914, thanks to the generous financial backing of a Rochester businessman, Hagen entered his second U.S. Open. That year it was held at the Midlothian Country Club outside Chicago.

The night before the opening round, Hagen dined on lobster and oysters at a Chicago restaurant. The next morning he was violently ill. At that time the Open was being played seventy-two holes over two days. Hagen did not think he could play thirty-six holes in his condition and considered withdrawing from the tournament. But not wanting to disappoint his backer, he persevered. With a green face complemented by a red bandana, he gingerly stepped onto the first tee on schedule.

Hagen opened with an excellent four-under-par 68 that placed him in the lead by one stroke over Frances Ouimet. In his afternoon round, Hagen shot a 74, which was good enough to keep him in the lead by one stroke. Ouimet fell off the pace in his second round, and Tom McNamara now occupied second place. That evening Hagen decided to stick with a tried-and-true meal of steak and potatoes.

On day 2 Hagen played steadily in his morning round and expanded his lead to two strokes over McNamara. In the final round, McNamara faltered, and Hagen withstood a late charge from noted amateur Chick Evans to win by one stroke. En route to his victory, Hagen birdied the par-four eighteenth hole in all four rounds, a feat no Open champion had done before or since.

When Hagen returned home, he did not receive the hero's welcome he expected. Much to his dismay, the highbrow members of the Country Club of Rochester treated him as just a glorified servant. A dejected Hagan, who had once shown promise as a pitcher for a local semipro team, toyed for a while with the idea of getting out of golf and giving professional baseball a whirl.

During the next two years, Hagen finished tenth and seventh in the United States Open and claimed victories in two prestigious tournaments: the New York City area's Metropolitan Open at Garden City and the Western Open, which at that time was considered one of golf's major tournaments.

When approached about the position at Oakland Hills, Hagen balked. Despite his treatment at the country club, he felt comfortable in Rochester. On the other hand, family and friends encouraged him to consider the move. After several days of deliberation, he decided to accept the offer.

Over the next several years at Oakland Hills, Hagen received the treatment of a member instead of an employee. Away from the club, he moved about Detroit's social circles with a style and grace that defied his humble background and education.

The 1919 United States Open took place outside Boston, at the Brae Burn Country Club in West Newton. After three rounds Hagen occupied second place, but he trailed the leader, local favorite Mike Brady of Boston, by five strokes. But over the course of his final eighteen holes, the wheels on Brady's game began to wobble and almost came off the rims. Playing almost two hours ahead of Hagen, when Brady holed his last putt at the eighteenth green, it gave him a score of eight-over-par 80. News of Brady's collapse reached Hagen as he was teeing off on the tenth hole. Hagen smoked the back nine. At the eighteenth green he faced a ten-footer to win the title by one stroke. The putt tracked straight for the cup. But instead of falling, it ran around the cup's edge and spun out. An eighteen-hole playoff was set for Brady and Hagen the next day.

Since his move to Oakland Hills, Hagen had gained the reputation, deservingly so, of being quite the partier. This reputation would skyrocket to new heights as a result of his partying the night before his playoff with Brady. Hagen threw a bash at his hotel for a group of his friends, one of whom was the singer, and an excellent golfer in his own right, Al Jolson. At a point well past midnight, one of Hagen's guests suggested that he should consider going to bed and getting some sleep. No doubt, Brady had already been in bed for hours. "He may be in bed, but he ain't asleep," Hagen quipped, and he partied on for several more hours.

After the first hole the next day, it appeared that Hagen should have listened to his friend and gone to bed. He made a bogey, while Brady had a tap-in par. But from that point the match seesawed back and forth, until they reached the par-three eighth. There Hagen took command of the match when he birdied and Brady bogeyed.

With a two-shot lead at the seventeenth tee, things looked good for Hagen, until he hit his tee shot, a horrific slice that led to a bogey. Brady parred the hole to shave Hagen's lead to one. With honors at the par-four eighteenth, Brady crushed his drive straight down the middle. At this point it appeared that Hagen's late-night partying had caught up with him, as he made another miserable swing from the tee.

This time he topped his drive, and he was left with over 220 yards to reach the green with his second shot. Hagen slammed a two-wood and almost got home. Brady helped him out by missing the green with his approach. Both golfers had chip shots from about 10 yards off the green. Brady almost holed his chip and then tapped in for par. Hagen's chip was only average, and he left himself a four-foot knee knocker for the win. He drained it.

After the golf season ended that year, the proud members of Oakland Hills threw a big banquet in Hagen's honor for his U.S. Open win. At the dinner Hagen received rousing applause as he rose and went to the dais to speak. He gave a gracious and heartfelt speech, thanking the members for their great support. Then he floored his audience by announcing his resignation as the club's pro—to become golf's first touring professional unaffiliated with a club, a status he would be alone in for several years.

FROM A HOSPITAL BED IN SANTA MONICA

Gene Sarazen was coming off his best year ever, having won both the United States Open and the British Open in 1932. A close second to his skill as a golfer was his skill as a publicity hound. In the winter of 1933, he pulled off his biggest publicity grab ever. Like his unforgettable double eagle shot at Augusta National two years later, it would be pulled off from a difficult lie—a hospital bed in Santa Monica, California.

Gene had made the three-day trip from the East Coast shortly after New Year's Day, arriving just in time to play in the Los Angeles Open. After two rounds he was forced to withdraw because he wasn't feeling well. The next day he checked into a nearby hospital in Santa Monica, where it was determined he had a case of the flu.

A few days later he granted an interview to an Associated Press reporter from his hospital bed. In the interview, which ran in papers nationwide, Gene declared that golf "had gotten too tame" and he had just the idea to give it some new energy. His brainchild was to widen the cup from its current width of 4.25 inches to 8. With the hole almost doubled in size, he was sure the weekend golfers' and the pros' enjoyment of the game would increase by leaps and bounds.

Had this proposal been brought forward by anyone but the defending U.S. Open and British Open champion, it is unlikely that it would have gotten off the ground. But because it was Gene Sarazen, it did. And for a publicity hound like Gene, it was manna from heaven and more, as it was a story that would keep his name in the forefront of the press for almost six weeks. A few days after the interview was published, Gene's voice was reduced to a whisper as his doctors decided that his tonsils had to go, but his eight-inch cup idea was making an abundance of noise, both pro and con.

On the plus side, a course in Kansas City found it had a set of posthole diggers with the exact width that was needed and turned its back nine into a testing ground for the eight-inch cup. A host of the club players participated in the test, and most were very positive about the idea, as many believed the enlarged cups had lowered their score for those nine holes by two to three strokes.

On the negative side, and on the same day of the Kansas City test, another test trial of the idea took place at one of golf's most prestigious locales, Pinehurst No. 2 in Pinehurst, North Carolina. Taking part in the experiment were several prominent names in the game of golf. They were famed golf course designer Donald Ross; Richard S. Tufts, the son of the founder of Pinehurst Golf Resort and its current director and a future president of the United States Golf Association; and William Clark Fownes Jr., the principal owner of the Oakmont Country Club, a former U.S. Amateur champion, and a former president of the United States Golf Association. This group's take was the polar opposite of the Kansas City group. After the Pinehurst trial, they were all thumbs down.

Among Sarazen's tournament-playing contemporaries, support for the idea was in the 30 to 35 percent category. Among the remaining 65 to 70 percent, responses ranged from lukewarm to hearty opposition. The *New York Times* reported that when he was asked for his opinion, Albert R. Gates, administrator for the PGA, refused to give any credence to the idea. He said, "I think Gene is kidding the public a bit."

Where Gene's proposal seemed to strike a nerve was among the elder statesmen of the game in Great Britain. Six-time British Open champion Harry Vardon said of Gene's idea, "Tommyrot!" Sandy Herd, the winner of the 1902 British Open, deemed the idea "farcical." He declared, "You would have to be blind to miss an eight-inch cup."

The criticism of his idea did not sit well with Gene. Still in the hospital, he put in a call, which would be chronicled the next day in the *Los Angeles Times*, to the Associated Press office in Los Angeles. When a reporter answered the phone, Gene said, "This is Sarazen in rebuttal."

"In what?" the reporter asked.

"Rebuttal. It is a legal word [that] means a comeback. Sort of a counterpunch."

"What do you propose to rebut?"

"Some of my friends who are firing at me for my suggestion that the golf cups be increased to eight inches. From the papers, some of them seem to think I'm loony."

"Go ahead."

"Well, take the British. I see I can't get any support there. Well, I am not surprised for I did not expect my friends on the other side would agree with me in any proposal for a change in the game of golf. My answer to that is that in the old days we fought with knives and swords and now we fight with airplanes.

"A lot of games have been better for changes. In baseball, once upon a time a batter was out if a fielder caught a ball on the first bounce but not anymore.

"I noticed Pinehurst didn't think much of the big cup. The answer to that is they have sand greens there. A twelve-inch cup wouldn't make any difference on a sand green."

In response to the dismissive comment from Gates, the administrator of the PGA, Gene said: "Mr. Gates thinks I am kidding the public. I am not kidding anybody."

Gene welcomed all the tests that were being scheduled by clubs across the country. But he believed the real test would come when the cups were used by professionals in the seventy-two-hole tournament he was planning for the first week in March in Miami.

The day after his call to the Associated Press, Gene was released from the hospital and traveled to Miami. Meanwhile, tests were continuing across the country.

Within a few days after arriving in Miami, Gene was out on the practice green, putting at an eight-inch cup. After several days of practice, he concluded that an eight-inch cup was just a little too large—a six-inch cup was the way to go, and that would be the size used in the upcoming enlarged cup tournament.

A week later, with six-inch cups in place, the Miami-Biltmore hosted what was called "the Florida Year-Round Club $5,000 Open." Its field of 102 included almost all of the big-name players. After the end of day 1, the scores were good but not the super-low scores that many were expecting. Al Espinosa and Willie McFarlane shared the lead at four-under 67. Gene struggled with the bigger target and shot 76.

On day 2 the scores overall ticked a little higher, except for the card turned in by Paul Runyan. He was considered one of the game's best putters and best player with pitches and chips. He shot a seven-under-par 64 to take a one-shot lead. The high point of his round came when he holed an eighty-yard shot.

Rounds 3 and 4 were played on the last day of the tournament. Again, the only player who excelled was Runyan. He posted rounds of 65 and 68 to take the event by ten strokes. Except for Runyan, no one else in the field had made any noise with their putting. Gene had rallied over the last thirty-six holes, with rounds of 67 and 68.

Scores were considered to be one to two strokes better per round, but the excitement Gene felt sure would come with the larger cups never materialized.

In interviews with the participants after the tournament, the pros did not care for the enlarged cups. Many of the best putters in the field had the most problems with them. They found it difficult to find a central spot to focus on with such a large target. Gene tried to put a different spin on the situation. He argued that a single tournament was not a fair test and that three or four more would be needed.

Gene could not get his call for more tournaments off the ground. And the idea seemed to die as quickly as it had taken off when Gene first proposed it.

TWO TRAILBLAZERS NEED ASSISTANCE WITH FINDING A PLACE TO PLAY

When Dwight Eisenhower was in the White House, he teed it up anywhere he wanted to: Congressional Country Club, Burning Tree, Cypress Point, the Newport Country Club, and of course, Augusta National. For the most part this applied to every other avid golfer on his staff as well, except for E. Frederic Morrow, the first Black person ever to hold an executive position on the White House staff.

In the summer of 1952, Morrow, a native of Hackensack, New Jersey, and a graduate of Rutgers University Law School, took a leave of absence from his position in the Public Affairs Department of Columbia Broadcasting System (CBS) to work on Eisenhower's presidential campaign. Morrow, who had climbed his way up in the army from a private to a major, impressed several of Eisenhower's top aides with his efforts for the campaign. After Eisenhower's big election win over Adlai Stevenson, Morrow was told that there would be a position for him at the White House. But when the dust had settled after the election, no firm offer was ever tendered, and Morrow ended up taking a position with the Department of Commerce.

Finally, almost two years after the election, an offer came for him to join the White House staff. Although his work at the Commerce Department had been challenging and rewarding, he was eager to accept the huge challenges and responsibilities of being the first Black person to serve in that capacity.

Morrow's official position was administrative officer for special projects, but his actual role would be to serve as the administration's sounding board on civil rights matters and as its liaison with the Black community.

Morrow enjoyed playing golf almost as much as Eisenhower. The demands of his new position, however, gave him very little time to play; plus, he faced the same challenges as many other Black golfers in the country, and that was finding a course that would allow him to play. Unfortunately, he never received an invitation from Eisenhower to join him for a round.

Morrow did receive one invitation from Eisenhower that he would never forget. On a trip to Chicago in the fall of 1956, he was trying to slip in a round of golf with some friends, but a message delivered to him on the course sent him scurrying back to Washington. Eisenhower wanted him to be a part of his traveling party on a trip to New York City. It was Morrow's first ride on *Air Force One*, and it was quite an experience for him. The presidential party's destination was not Wall Street or the United Nations; it was a much more important venue than that. They were headed for Ebbets Field to attend the first game of the World Series between the Brooklyn Dodgers and the New York Yankees.

On the field that day for the Dodgers was Jackie Robinson, who had broken baseball's racial barrier nine years earlier. He would meet Morrow at an NAACP dinner in White Plains, New York, several months later, and the two would become good friends.

Robinson, too, was hooked on golf and despite all of his fame encountered the same difficulties as many Black Americans when it came to finding a place to play. Once Morrow went up to Robinson's home in Stamford, Connecticut, for a weekend of golf. Robinson had been invited to join a country club nearby, but when several members complained, he decided against joining. For their golf that weekend, Robinson prevailed upon a friend at ABC Television, who got the two tee times at the Fenwick Country Club in White Plains, New York.

A TRIUMPHANT COMEBACK

In May 1965 forty-year-old Dick Mayer became golf's comeback story of the year, when he chipped in for a birdie from thirty-five yards on the final hole in the New Orleans Open to squeeze out a one-shot victory over Bruce Devlin. Mayer had been golf's golden boy in 1957, winning the U.S. Open and the Tam O'Shanter in Chicago, which paid golf's biggest purse. A few years later, he lost his confidence and passion for the game and dropped off the tour. He tried working on Wall Street, selling insurance, and selling cars. In early 1965 he decided to give golf another try.

At the seventy-second hole at New Orleans, it appeared Mayer was in danger of coming up just short of a win. Playing with his fellow coleader, Bruce Devlin, he hit his drive into the rough. From there he struck his approach shot heavy, and it came up thirty-five yards short of the pin. Devlin was in good position off the tee. His approach shot came to rest just six feet from the hole.

On his third shot, the chain-smoking Mayer took a long drag from his cigarette and then flipped it on the ground. He addressed his ball and, with a smooth motion that belied the situation, executed his chip. He was thirty feet from the putting surface and another seventy-five feet from the hole. His ball landed one-third of the way to its target and tracked dead online into the cup for birdie. Devlin's putt for a birdie and a tie was wide by a half-inch.

MICHELLE GETS HER MAJOR

When Michelle Wie West won the 2014 Women's United States Open at Pinehurst, no one had thought it would take so long or that this would be her only major of the five tournaments she would win as a professional.

Michelle's career had been launched over a decade earlier amid unprecedented hype and attention. She displayed incredible talent at an early age and was heralded as a female version of Tiger Woods, and she was thought to be on her way to becoming the greatest female golfer ever.

It was hard to argue against that assessment. She played in her first LPGA event when she was twelve. When she was fourteen she began accepting sponsor's exemptions to tee it up against the opposite sex in PGA Tour events.

Over the next four years, she would play in eight. Her best performance was in the Sony Open in her native state of Hawaii, where she shot rounds of 72 and 68 and missed making the thirty-six-hole cut by one stroke. In an interview with Steve Kroft in a segment of CBS's Sixty Minutes Michelle let it be known that one of her goals was to play in the Masters. But she was not too keen about putting on the green jacket. She considered it out of fashion.

Michelle began her golf journey at age four and was introduced to the game by her parents, who both emigrated to Hawaii from Korea. Her mother, Bo, a Honolulu realtor, had won South Korea's women's amateur golf championship four years before Michelle was born. Her father, B.J., a professor at the University of Hawaii, was pretty good on the golf course as well, getting his handicap down at one time to two.

A week before her sixteenth birthday in 2005, Michelle announced that she was turning professional. She signed sponsorship contracts with Nike and Sony reportedly worth more than $10 million per year.

Michelle's pro career got off to a rocky start. In her first tournament, the Samsung World Championship, she was disqualified when a *Sports Illustrated* reporter observed her take an incorrect drop and reported it to tournament officials. Soon after in another tournament, she was disqualified for a second time. This one was for a scorecard infraction. Moving forward there seemed to be more downs than ups. She went through a number of caddies and there was a nagging wrist injury. The prediction that she was going to be the female Tiger Woods soon dissipated.

Nine years later when the 2014 season got underway, Michelle's win total on Tour was just three, and no majors. But in the first major that year, the Kraft-Nabisco Championship at the Mission Hills Country Club in Rancho Mirage, California, she started strong and stayed near the top of the leaderboard for the first two rounds and when the third round was over she was in a tie for first place with the most recent young phenom to show up on tour, nineteen-year-old Lexi Thompson.

The final round turned out to be all Lexi. On a stretch of five holes on the front side, she recorded four birdies and was up by five on Michelle when they reached the tenth tee. Lexi went on to win by three strokes.

Two months later at the U.S. Open at Pinehurst, Michelle again put together three strong rounds and when she teed off in the final round she was tied with Amy Yang for the lead. Yang faded and midway through the back nine Michelle was in front by three strokes. It appeared she was on the verge of finally capturing a major. But things went wrong at the long par-four sixteenth hole. An errant second shot forced her to take a penalty shot for an unplayable lie. The next shot left her thirty-five feet from the pin. Her putt for bogey raced by the hole and left her a stress-loaded five-footer for double-bogey, which she rolled into the cup.

Michelle's lead was down to one over Stacey Lewis, who had started the day six strokes off the pace but had recorded eight birdies in her round on the way to a four-under-par 66. She had already finished and was on the practice range keeping loose in hopes of a playoff opportunity.

Those hopes would be short-lived. At the par-three seventeenth, Michelle rolled in a twenty-five-footer for birdie to push her lead to two. She parred eighteen and that long awaited major win was hers.

Addressing the media afterward, Michelle said this with the trophy at her side: "I think the fact that I struggled so much, the fact that I kind of went through a hard period of my life, the fact that this trophy is right next to me, it means so much more to me than it ever would have when I was fifteen."

Michelle's next and last win came in the 2018 HSBC Women's World Championship in Singapore. In 2019 she married Jonnie West, the director of Basketball Operations for the Golden State Warriors and the son of NBA legend Jerry West. She gave birth to a daughter in 2020. After the 2022 Women's U.S. Open at Pebble Beach, Michelle announced she was stepping away from the game.

TWELVE GOLFERS PLAY IT OFF FOR ELEVEN SPOTS

At the 1913 U.S. Amateur at Garden City, New Jersey, two qualifying rounds were held. The first round included all 140 entries with the lowest 64 scorers advancing to the second day. On the second day, the slate would be wiped clean and the low 32 out of the 64 would advance into match play for the championship.

The second day of qualifying produced one of the most unusual sites ever at a USGA championship, as twelve golfers were required to play the same hole at the same time.

When the second eighteen-hole qualifying round concluded, there was a major log jam. Twelve golfers had tied for the last eleven spots. So a playoff had to be conducted and the entire dozen trouped back to the first tee.

Some big names were in the twelve: Jerry Travers, the defending champion; Robert Scott, the current president of the United States Golf Association; and Heinrich Schmidt.

Schmidt struggled the first day, making the field of sixty-four by just one stroke. He looked like a different golfer than the one who had captured the golfing world's attention a few months earlier. The twenty-two-year-old recent college graduate, who had been the amateur champion of Massachusetts the year before, had journeyed across the Atlantic to play in the British Amateur at the Old Course at St. Andrews. As the matches rolled on, Schmidt continued to advance and became a gallery favorite.

At that time, the golfers of Great Britain were upholding the long-standing tradition of wearing coats while on the course, even in the hottest weather. Schmidt warmed the galleries to his cause even further by honoring that long-standing tradition by wearing in all his matches what one observer described as "the thickest of tweed suits."

With each match he won, Schmidt drew bigger and bigger crowds, and when he won his fifth match, many thought that would be it for Schmidt, as in his sixth match he had to face the most accomplished golfer in Great Britain: Harold Hilton. He was a three-time winner of this event and had won the British Open twice.

In their match, Schmidt, still wearing his thick tweed suit, displayed great poise. Nothing seemed to rattle him. He took his time over each stroke. And on the greens, he was exceedingly deliberate and he was matching Hilton shot for shot.

In those earlier matches most in the gallery were delighted to see Schmidt doing so well. He was a common working-class young man who had worked his way through college and now he was working his way through a field of British golfers that were by and large members of Great Britain's more affluent classes. But as the match unfolded against Hilton, they had not ever fathomed he could do this well. As it became evident, the unthinkable was very possible. An unheralded American golfer might just defeat Britain's foremost amateur and at, of all places, the empire's and world's shrine of golf.

After eighteen holes, the match was all square. So Hilton and Schmidt went back to the first tee for a playoff. Schmidt's birdie putt came up just short and Hilton then drained a twenty-five-footer for birdie to claim the match.

Hilton would win his next two matches to claim his fourth British Amateur title.

At the U.S. Amateur at Garden City, Schmidt drew an abundance of snickers from fellow competitors and spectators because, in the blazing sun of summer, he was wearing the thick tweed suit he had worn at St. Andrews. But no one was snickering after all twelve playoff participants had hit their drives at the first playoff hole. Schmidt was the longest and straightest of the lot.

Schmidt was the last to hit his approach shot. With several players in trouble, either from poor drives or poor second shots, Schmidt could play it safe and easily make the final thirty-two. The only trouble at the first hole was a bunker directly in front of the green. He hit a high-lofting shot for the heart of the green. It didn't make it. His ball plopped down in the bunker near its front edge.

The face of this bunker was not earth but wooden planks. Schmidt's blast out of the bunker wasn't high enough. It struck one of the planks and ricocheted backward, out into the fairway. Playing his fourth from the fairway, Schmidt still had a shot at tying several of the other participants with a decent pitch and a two-putt. But he put his fourth shot right back into the bunker. Finally, Schmidt put his fifth shot on the green and he still had a good chance of avoiding elimination. One other golfer, A. C. Ulmer, from Jacksonville, Florida, had also taken five blows to reach the putting surface. He was some sixty feet from the hole and Schmidt was well inside of him. If Schmidt could one-putt, he was in the field. If they both two-putted, he and Ulmer would continue the playoff.

Ulmer stared at the line of his putt for a few moments, and then he rolled it into the hole. Schmidt missed his putt for six. After having the best drive among twelve golfers, he finished dead last among the twelve and was eliminated.

TWO SAD PASSINGS

In March of 1925, sixty-year-old James Swan collapsed on a busy New York City street corner. He was rushed to Bellevue Hospital where he died a few hours later. The cause of death: exposure.

Swan had been among the first in a horde of Scottish golf professionals who came to the United States in the 1890s. He had given lessons on the grounds of Van Cortlandt Park years before the country's first public golf course would be constructed there. He was also one of the first golf professionals to serve at the country's first golf club, St. Andrew's in Yonkers.

Swan also laid out and supervised the construction of a number of courses, among them Elk Ridge Country Club in Baltimore, Quogue on Long Island, and the course at Princeton University in Princeton, New Jersey, where he would serve as the club's professional. While there he provided golf instruction to one former President of the United States, Grover Cleveland, and a future president, Woodrow Wilson.

Swan had fallen on hard times and was living on the streets at the time of his death. When he collapsed he was carrying no identification. The hospital staff did find a business card in one of his pockets for an executive with a firm in New York and asked this gentleman to come to the hospital and identify the body. He recognized the man to be Swan, who had given him golf instruction some fifteen years earlier.

Since he had no next of kin, Swan's body was going to be taken to Potter's Field for burial. But upon hearing the news of his death, the Professional Golf Association sent a representative to claim the body. They made arrangements for a funeral at a local mortuary and Swan's burial.

On a stormy August night in 1948 in Springfield, New Jersey, a homeless man entered the local police station and asked if he could spend the night in a cell. The sympathetic police officer on duty honored the man's request. The next morning, the homeless man was discovered dead in the cell. It would later be determined that the cause of his death was pneumonia.

The man's name was Cyril Walker. Nearly a quarter of a century earlier, his name had been splashed across the nation's sports pages because he had won the 1924 United States Open at the Oakland Hills Country Club in Birmingham, Michigan, a suburb northwest of Detroit. Walker was born in Manchester, England, and he was introduced to golf at the age of ten. By the time he was in his early twenties, he had developed a stellar game, despite his short height and slight build.

Walker emigrated to the United States in 1914 and worked as a club professional in New Jersey, first at the Shackamaxon Country Club and then at Englewood Golf Club in Englewood, New Jersey. He enjoyed moderate success as a player, winning the 1916 Indiana Open and the 1921 Pennsylvania Open. In the years 1921–23, he'd finished thirteenth, fortieth, and twenty-third in the U.S. Open. During his tournament play, he earned a very dubious distinction as he was given the title of "the slowest player ever known to the American golf links."

At the end of the third round in the 1924 Open, the 120-pound Walker seemed as surprised as everyone else that he was in a tie for the lead. The player with him atop the leaderboard was Bobby Jones, the tournament's defending champion. After nine holes in the final round, the two were still tied. Walker pulled away on the back nine to win by three strokes.

After his Open win, Walker started playing more tournaments and he grew increasingly unpopular with fellow players due to his slow play. He was known to examine even the smallest pebbles anywhere around his ball. He would check the wind, then check it a few more times for good measure. He would take up to a dozen practice swings before every shot.

The greatest example of Walker's disregard for pace of play came in the second round of the 1930 Los Angeles Open. Marshals had tried to speed him along, to no avail, and they disqualified him. Walker refused to quit playing and the police were called in and they removed him from the course.

Walker developed a serious drinking problem and became estranged from his wife and son. He soon disappeared from the tournament golf scene.

In 1940, sixteen years after his U.S. Open win, a reporter acting on a tip found Walker working as a caddie at the municipal course in Miami Beach, Florida, and living at a Salvation Army home, where lodging cost twenty-five cents each day.

At some point over the next eight years, Walker made his way back to New Jersey and worked for a while as a part-time dishwasher in Hackensack, and lived at the YMCA. Not much is known about the remainder of his final years.

WALTER HAGEN'S A VICTIM OF A CRIME

In 1927 Walter Hagen made headlines when he swore out a warrant for the arrest of his caddie, James McDonald. Two years earlier Hagen had made big news when he hired McDonald and became the first touring professional to have a full-time caddie. And it was indeed full-time, as Hagen took McDonald with him overseas to the British Open.

By all accounts the two had a good relationship, but when Hagen returned to his apartment in Hollywood, Florida, one evening in mid-March 1927, he discovered it had been ransacked. Hagen soon learned that McDonald had gained entry to his apartment from the property's manager under false pretenses. Gone were most of the best-dressed golfer in the country's wardrobe, jewelry, and a sizable amount of cash.

Shortly after the theft, Hagen learned his apartment was not the only score McDonald, who was never apprehended, had made. He had also scammed several of Hagen's acquaintances out of money.

A MARATHON STRETCH OF GOLF

Jimmy Demaret teed it up for eleven straight days in the winter of 1949. And in that stretch, he was twice in playoffs against the great Ben Hogan. Demaret's marathon streak began in Long Beach, California, at the Long Beach Open. The start of that event was delayed one day because of rain. Hogan and Demaret were tied for the lead when it wrapped up on Monday.

At this time on tour, ties were resolved with an eighteen-hole playoff, so Demaret and Hogan squared off on Tuesday. Hogan prevailed, shooting a five-under-par 67 to Demaret's 69.

Immediately after their playoff, Demaret and Hogan headed for the tour's next stop, the Phoenix Open. Hogan took the next day off, but Demaret honored a commitment to play in that event's pro-am. When the tournament's four rounds wrapped up on Sunday, Demaret and Hogan were again tied for the top spot.

If anyone could handle back-to-back playoffs with the iron-willed and stoic Hogan, it was Demaret. Always adorned in flamboyant, colorful attire, he ambled over the course with the nonchalance of a golfer who didn't care if he broke 100. Off the course he loved to hit the nightclub circuit at the stops on tour, often singing and doing stand-up comedy. In the Phoenix playoff, he came out on top with a four-under 67 to Hogan's one under 70.

Two days after the playoff, while driving from Phoenix to his home in Fort Worth, Hogan was involved in a head-on crash with a Greyhound bus that almost took his life.

GOLF AND THE COLD WAR, PART 1

The Cold War developed after World War II between the United States and the Soviet Union and their respective allies. It was being waged on political, economic, and propaganda fronts.

In the summer of 1959, President Eisenhower sought to cool down the red-hot Cold War and invited Soviet premier Nikita Khrushchev to the United States. Khrushchev quickly accepted the invitation.

The United States allies were caught off guard by the announcement, so Eisenhower chose to make a quick trip to Europe before Khrushchev's scheduled mid-September visit to ease the anxiety of the leaders in Great Britain, West Germany, and France.

The first stop was a meeting with British prime minister Harold Macmillan. While in London Eisenhower stayed at Winfield House, the estate Woolworth heiress Betty Hutton had donated to the United States after World War II for use as the American ambassador to Great Britain's official residence. Eisenhower found the huge back lawn of the estate too inviting to resist. He directed his personal physician, Dr. Howard Snyder, to pace off 150 yards, and then stand there and serve as a target so Eisenhower and Jock Whitney, the Augusta National member whom Eisenhower had appointed ambassador to Great Britain, could practice some golf shots with their irons. Snyder managed to survive the session without getting struck.

From Great Britain, it was on to West Germany to meet with its chancellor, Konrad Adenauer, and then to France for talks with its president, Charles de Gaulle. After stroking his allies about his forthcoming talks with Khrushchev, Eisenhower decided he wanted to take some strokes on a golf course, so he made a side trip to Scotland.

In 1945 the owner of one of Scotland's most famous castles, Culzean, donated it to the country's National Trust. Constructed in the late eighteenth century, the grand, three-story castle is located on Scotland's Ayrshire Coast. There was one proviso attached to the donation by its owner, and that was, in consideration for his efforts in securing victory in World War II, Eisenhower would be granted use of the castle's third-floor apartment for life. With the Turnberry Golf Course, a future site of four British Opens, located just down the road from the castle, Eisenhower thought it would be a good place for a short layover.

Before leaving Paris, Eisenhower called fellow Augusta National members Bill Robinson and Pete Jones in New York City. He requested that they join him on the links in Scotland. They both dropped what plans they had and scrambled to make flight arrangements that would allow them to arrive in time to play the next day.

Eisenhower flew on to Scotland to get in a round that afternoon. He arrived at the castle, changed clothes, and headed over to the Turnberry Golf Club. Boosted by a birdie on a par five, he shot a very respectable 42 on the front side. His whirlwind travel schedule, and possibly his sixty-nine-year-old body, began to tell on him on the backside, as the wheels on his game began to wobble a bit. But he still reached the eighteenth tee needing only a double-bogey six to break 90.

Eisenhower made the final hole a real adventure. He sculled his drive, and it went nowhere. He then hit a decent recovery fairway wood shot but followed it with a poor iron shot that ended up in a greenside bunker. His bunker shot barely made it onto the green, but he managed to two-putt for a six and a score of 89. Eisenhower's play with Robinson and

Jones over the next two days was more solid, as he scored in the mid-80s for both rounds.

Khrushchev arrived in Washington DC soon after Eisenhower's return from Scotland, and they had some preliminary discussions at the White House. Khrushchev then embarked on a tour of the country, visiting New York City, Iowa farms, and Hollywood. He was bitterly disappointed in California when his request to visit Disneyland was turned down for security reasons. His pain over that denial, however, was soothed over when he was afforded the opportunity to meet Hollywood's hottest sex symbol, Marilyn Monroe. She was quite a sight to behold, having been instructed to wear the tightest-fitting dress she owned for the good of Soviet-American relations.

Khrushchev wrapped up his ten-day visit by returning to Washington. He and Eisenhower were helicoptered to Camp David for two days of intense talks. On the way out of the capital, Eisenhower gave him an aerial view of Burning Tree Golf Club. Khrushchev would later write about that moment, stating: "We flew over a big green field where he told me he played golf. He asked me whether I liked the sport, and I didn't have the slightest idea what it was all about. He told me it was a very healthy sport."

Despite neither leader being up to par—Khrushchev had trouble sleeping during his tour, and Eisenhower was fighting a severe cold he had caught on the links in Scotland—the spirit of their talks raised world expectations dramatically over the possibility of peaceful coexistence between the two superpowers.

Eisenhower agreed to visit the USSR in the summer of 1960. Khrushchev left the United States all aglow and went back to Russia and immediately began to plan for Eisenhower's visit. He planned to spare no expense to make his newfound friend feel welcome when he visited his country. On a magnificent pine bluff overlooking a lake, he was going to build a grand house for Eisenhower's use during his stay. His other good American friend, Llewellyn Thompson, the United States ambassador to the Soviet Union, had also convinced him that not having a golf course in the Soviet Union hurt the country's prestige. Preparations were underway to build a course and have it ready in time for Eisenhower to play when he arrived. There were even reports that Khrushchev was going to take some lessons so he could play a few holes with Eisenhower during his visit.

The cold Eisenhower had picked up in Scotland lingered, and two weeks after Khrushchev departed, he decided that warm air, sunshine, and golf were the prescription he needed. Unfortunately, Augusta National was only open from November through April and was not scheduled to open up for another month, so he opted for a healing trip to Palm Springs, California, instead. But after an eight-day stay, he returned to Washington still with a cold. The malady continued to persist, and on October 20 Eisenhower called up Augusta National chairman Cliff Roberts at his office in New York City and asked if he could open up Augusta National early for him. Roberts agreed to do it.

Eisenhower stayed for four days. Roberts described the four days as the worst stretch of weather Eisenhower ever experienced at Augusta, each of the days being cloudy and cool, with occasional showers. Eisenhower was undaunted by the elements, however, and took the cure. He played eighteen holes on the first day, twenty-seven on the second day, thirty-six on the third day, and eighteen on the last day. When Eisenhower departed Augusta, his cold was gone.

GOLF AND THE COLD WAR, PART 2

When Eisenhower returned to Washington DC from his stay at Augusta National, his primary focus was on his upcoming trip to the Soviet Union that summer. There had been a story in the *New York Times* in early January that hinted that the construction of the golf course there was coming along. If Eisenhower had wanted to check on the progress himself, he certainly had the means to do so.

As it had on most Americans, Pearl Harbor had had a deep effect on Eisenhower. He believed that it was imperative to know what one's biggest adversary was up to militarily. Just over sixty days after Eisenhower took office, Soviet premier Joseph Stalin died and the whole Russian hierarchy was in turmoil, and the need for solid intelligence increased dramatically. To this end, Eisenhower signed off on the development of the high-altitude spy plane—the U-2—in November 1954.

The scientists and engineers given the task of taking the plane from the drawing board to the skies over the Soviet Union were assigned office space in the Executive Office Building next to the White House. They worked practically around the clock to get the project off the ground.

During late afternoon breaks from their labor, they would often look out their office window and see Eisenhower working on his eight-iron shots on the South Lawn.

After the plans were completed at the Executive Office Building, the plane was secretly built by the Lockheed Corporation in California. A Lockheed test pilot was given the task of finding a suitable location for the testing of the plane. He picked a remote spot near Grooms Lake, Nevada. It was located on the edge of the Nevada nuclear test site. This location would later become known as "Area 51."

In May 1956 the first U-2 made its maiden flight over Communist-occupied territory and was an immediate success. The Soviets immediately detected that they were being overflown, but they did not have a missile capable of shooting down the high-flying intruder.

On Sunday, April 11, 1960, Eisenhower was itching to get down to Augusta National for his annual week-after-the-Masters vacation. How soon he would be able to scratch that itch would depend on a former member of the United States Coast Guard he was watching on his television at the White House. The individual whose actions the president of the United States was so keenly interested in was Arnold Palmer.

Palmer was trying to win the Masters for the second time. He had led the first three rounds of the tournament, but as he prepared to play his approach shot to the par-four eighteenth, he was in a tie with Ken Venturi, who had already finished his round. If Palmer parred the hole, he and Venturi would go at each other in an eighteen-hole playoff the following day and Eisenhower's Augusta vacation would be delayed for twenty-four hours. Palmer's six-iron approach shot produced a loud roar at the eighteenth green and a loud cheer at the White House, as it came to rest just six feet from the hole. Palmer then drilled his putt into the cup for a birdie and the win, freeing up the president of the United States to depart for his favorite golf haven.

Eisenhower played a lot of shots during his April stay at Augusta and probably took a few mulligans. For those not familiar with the term, a mulligan is when a golfer is given the opportunity to replay a poor shot without penalty. In early April, Eisenhower made a decision that would have to be the one over all other decisions he made during his presidency for which he would have loved to have been granted a mulligan.

The U-2 spy plane was getting its job done, and very soon the United States would have satellite capability that could take its place. The Soviets were still believed not to have a missile capable of hitting the U-2. Each mission of the U-2 had to be signed off on by Eisenhower, and he was getting more than a little edgy about the operation. He knew the situation with the Russian missile program would not last forever. There was a summit meeting with Khrushchev scheduled in Paris in May, and with his trip to the Soviet Union to take place later in the summer, Eisenhower was reluctant to authorize more U-2 flights.

Shortly before his mid-April trip to Augusta, the CIA had pressed Eisenhower for one more U-2 run over the Soviet Union. He grudgingly approved the mission but stipulated that it had to be completed in two weeks. Unfortunately, bad weather over the Soviet Union kept the U-2 on the ground, and the two-week window for the flight expired. On April 25, 1960, four days after Eisenhower returned from Augusta, the CIA requested an extension on the mission, and Eisenhower gave them an additional seven days to conduct the flight.

On Sunday morning, May 1, Eisenhower and his close friend George Allen had been driven from Camp David to Gettysburg to play golf, but because of rain, they never got off the first tee. Approximately ten hours earlier, pilot Gary Powers and his U-2 spy plane had been delayed on the runway at an air base in Turkey for almost an hour. Unfortunately for Eisenhower, Powers did get off, and thanks to the recently improved capability of the Russian military's missile program, he was now on the ground in the Soviet Union, in custody. Eisenhower and Allen had returned to Camp David from Gettysburg. They then did some skeet shooting. During the shooting session, Eisenhower received word that Powers's U-2 was overdue and most likely down in the Soviet Union.

Eisenhower had always been told that the U-2, despite its high-flying capability, was a very fragile bird and that if one were ever hit by a missile, the pilot and the equipment on board would never survive. Since Eisenhower and his team did not know for sure what had happened to the plane, they had the National Aeronautical and Space Administration issue a press release stating one of their weather planes was missing on a flight that had taken place near the Russian border. The release also stated that during the last radio contact with the plane, the pilot had reported having trouble with his oxygen supply.

Khrushchev was laughing while Eisenhower and his team were digging themselves into a very big hole. For several days he kept quiet about the fact that they had shot down the U-2 and had Powers in their custody, while Eisenhower kept up his normal work and golf routines. It appeared to Eisenhower that he was going to get out of the situation without any major damage. Then Khrushchev dropped the bomb. He announced to the world that they had shot down the plane and that the pilot was alive and in Soviet custody. Eisenhower had to admit to the U-2's activities over the last five years and that he had attempted to mislead the country and the world with the weather plane story.

Over the next ten days before the summit meeting in Paris, Khrushchev was bashing Eisenhower in the press, charging repeatedly that Eisenhower cared more about golf than world peace. Eisenhower was still determined to go to the summit, hoping he could somehow reconstruct a dialogue with Khrushchev. When Eisenhower got to Paris, he knew Khrushchev was going to try to make him grovel, and he hoped he would get a chance to speak first, so he could attempt to put his own slant on the situation. But when the meeting started, Khrushchev got the jump on him, quickly rising to his feet, railing against Eisenhower and the United States from what appeared to be a mountain of prepared text. He concluded his long tirade by stating that the summit should be postponed for six to eight months—by which time Eisenhower would be not a lame duck but a political dead duck—and that he was withdrawing his invitation to Eisenhower. He was no longer welcome in the Soviet Union. Despite resuscitation efforts by the French and British, the summit meeting collapsed, and a disheartened Eisenhower returned home.

TIGER PUTS ON A STAGGERING SPECTACLE, AND NICKLAUS BOWS OUT

Tiger Woods disappeared from the rest of the field's radar screens as he flew into never-before-seen heights and claimed his first United States Open title in June 2000. This was the United States Open's one hundredth anniversary, and Tiger's performance was a fitting tribute to its centennial celebration. He shot rounds of 65, 69, 71, and 67. His twelve-under-par 272 was the first time a player had finished in double digits under par in the event.

The two players who tied for second, Miguel Angel Jimenez and Ernie Els, finished at three over par, fifteen strokes behind Tiger. This fifteen-stroke margin of victory surpassed the thirteen-shot record margin for a major championship set by Old Tom Morris at the 1862 British Open Championship at Prestwick. Woods's aggregate of 272 tied what was then the lowest score in a U.S. Open, set by Jack Nicklaus and Lee Janzen, both achieved on par-seventy courses. Pebble Beach is a par seventy-two.

Tiger, who had been playing Pebble Beach since he was thirteen, had arrived as the odds-on favorite and with good reason. He had won twelve of his previous twenty-three tournaments, including the last five in a row.

One of those wins had come at Pebble Beach just a few months earlier, when he stormed from a seven-shot deficit with seven holes to play to win by a shot in the AT&T Pebble Beach National Pro-Am.

Jack Nicklaus was in the field, making his forty-fourth and last appearance in a United States Open. He did not make the cut, shooting rounds of 73 and 82.

Payne Stewart, the defending champion, had tragically died in a plane crash in late October 1999. On the afternoon of the day before the opening round, some forty PGA Tour players hit balls into the Pacific in a poignant tribute to Payne.

As the defending champion, Payne would have been in the opening group, with British Open champion Paul Lawrie and U.S. Amateur champion David Gossett. Nicklaus took his place in the group.

HOLLYWOOD'S HUSTLER

It was a warm July afternoon in Los Angeles in 1937. The city's attention, like the rest of America's, was focused on the forty-eight-hour-old search in the Pacific for the missing Amelia Earhart. On a busy boulevard just outside Hollywood, a seven-year search ended when a black-and-white police car pulled up alongside an expensive roadster being driven by John Montague and signaled for him to pull over.

The 1930s was Hollywood's heyday. Movies were never bigger, and the major players were the likes of Katharine Hepburn, Clark Gable, Jimmy Cagney, and Howard Hughes. And it seemed new stars were being discovered in Hollywood left and right. Lana Turner cut class at Hollywood High and ducked into a teen hangout for a Coke, where she caught an agent's eye and soon became famous as the silver screen's "sweater girl." The lovely Ellen Drew was discovered scooping ice cream on Hollywood Boulevard and appeared in twelve films in twelve months. Fred MacMurray was playing the saxophone in an orchestra when a studio executive saw him clowning around during a break and decided he had potential in front of a camera.

One studio decided "being discovered" would be a good story for a movie. The film's lead character was a starry-eyed farm girl who is discovered waitressing and almost overnight becomes Hollywood's top actress. The film's title was *A Star Is Born*.

The being discovered dream sent a multitude of young men and women swarming to the Hollywood area hoping to be the next big find. In this throng was a young man on the run from the law, and not being discovered was his number one priority. And this was not going to be easy for him because he had raw good looks; the smile, the self-assuredness, the charm and the mystique of Rhett Butler; the forearms of Popeye; the anger management issues of King Kong; and he played golf like he was Superman.

Of course, when you are on the run, a new name is always a good idea, and the young man chose "John Montague" as his. To generate some much-needed cash flow, he headed out to the area's municipal golf courses to do a little hustling. Armed with a heavily weighted driver that was light as a feather in his powerful grip, he slammed out colossal drives, which he followed up with an iron game that would have made William Tell envious of its accuracy. This enormously lethal one-two punch was always unleashed just when the time was right, and it left many of the municipal course's blue-collar clientele pondering where they were going to find the money to pay their rent.

A short distance from LA's municipal courses was a course in a different universe—the Lakeside Golf Club in North Hollywood. It was located just a short distance from both the Universal and Warner Brothers studios, and its membership roster read like a marquee of the movie industry's biggest names, with the likes of Bing Crosby, Johnny Weissmuller, Humphrey Bogart, Oliver Hardy, and W. C. Fields.

A Lakeside member who was a prominent real estate developer heard about Montague's golfing prowess and invited him out to Lakeside to be his partner in a match. This gentleman must have been looking to have a little fun with a couple of his fellow Lakesiders because they were told his guest was a ten handicap. This ruse had a very short life, as the match had hardly begun before the opponents were screaming ringer. And although play continued, all bets were canceled. But the fuse had been ignited on one of the most intriguing stories in Hollywood history.

Mr. Montague was soon asked back out to Lakeside on several more occasions to display his talents to other members. His performances in these return engagements were Oscar-like in the "Shock and Awe" category, and it wasn't very long before he received an invitation to join the club.

The Lakeside membership embraced their newest member like he was Tinseltown's answer to Bobby Jones, and Montague provided plenty of justification to support this golf god–like treatment. On a junket up to Pebble Beach with some of his fellow Lakesiders, Montague's drive on the fourteenth hole was 50 yards longer than Bobby Jones's had been when he reached that 500-yard par five with a driver and a three-wood in the 1928 U.S. Amateur. On his second shot, Montague went with a mid-iron and went over the green.

Montague also had the complete package as a trick-shot artist. To demonstrate the amount of clubhead speed he could generate, he would have his caddie lay on his back with a match in his teeth. He then would address a spot just above the match and take a full swing, igniting the match without disturbing its position in the extremely trusting caddie's mouth. He also could consistently blast shots from buried lies in a greenside bunker to within gimme range using a two-wood. Another favorite stunt was to bury a ball in the fairway forty yards from the green and then blast it onto the putting surface with a massive swing with a nine-iron.

Montague's trick shots weren't confined to the golf course. He once won a bet that he couldn't hit a golf ball over a fourteen-story building, and at a cocktail party he picked up some cash by successfully pitching a ball into a glass that was on a fireplace mantel.

The most famous example of Montague's wizardry came at the expense of Bing Crosby. Crosby had been one of the first Lakeside members to take a shine to Montague, and the two were involved in frequent matches. One afternoon in the club bar after a round, Crosby, who had been club champion at Lakeside several times and would later make the field for the British Amateur, was bemoaning the fact that Montague had not given him enough strokes. Montague soon grew tired of Crosby's whining and blurted out, "I could beat you using a baseball bat, a shovel, and rake as clubs." Crosby jumped on the challenge, and a wager—accounts of the bet's size range, from $5 to $1,000—was set.

Twenty minutes later, Montague and Crosby were back in the bar after playing just one hole. On that hole, which was a par four, Montague used the bat for his tee shot and almost drove the green. His ball came to rest in a greenside bunker. From there he used the shovel and put his ball six feet from the hole. A few moments later, he said, "That's good pal," as he tapped the knee knocker Crosby had left himself for par back to him. Montague surveyed his putt briefly and then, using the handle of the rake like a pool cue, ran his ball into the cup for a birdie. An extremely dumbfounded Crosby conceded the match at that point and headed back to the bar.

The non-golf exploits of Montague also caused plenty of headshaking on his friend's part. If he wasn't on the golf course during the day, you would most likely find him at the Santa Anita racetrack, where he won just as easily as he did at golf. Montague consumed massive amounts of alcohol but never displayed any hint of intoxication. He required very little sleep, and his record for going without it was five days.

Montague's behavior when it came to women was definitely out of the ordinary in the Hollywood sense. With the host of beauties that either ran with or were attempting to gain access to his social circles, there were unlimited opportunities for dalliances, but he was always the gentleman's gentleman. He even requested that his cohorts not discuss their liaisons in his presence.

The only problem area for Montague was anger management. He could get more than a little testy with minimal provocation. Once during a match at Pebble Beach in which Ty Cobb was on the opposing team, the always abrasive baseball great challenged the score of Montague's playing partner, and in a flash Montague was nose to nose with Cobb and told him to drop the subject. Cobb did. Actor George Bancroft was not as lucky as Cobb. The 240-pound Bancroft, who usually played mobster heavies on the screen, had an exchange of words with Montague in the Lakeside locker room, and the next thing he knew he had been crammed into a locker.

Montague's situation had to be enormously surreal for him. He had fled to Southern California with the hope of going unnoticed and had somehow hustled his way into the most difficult spot in America not to be noticed—Hollywood's fast lane. And while his friends basked in the flashes of photographers' cameras, Montague avoided cameras like Superman would avoid Kryptonite. Howard Hughes wore a fedora to bring himself luck. Montague wore a fedora to keep his luck from running out, with its snap-brim pulled way down to cover as much of his face as possible when he was in unfamiliar territory or around unfamiliar faces.

MORE HOLLYWOOD'S HUSTLER

A lovely platinum blonde was going to be responsible for starting the clock ticking toward John Montague being found out. Her name was Florence Rice, and after some limited success on Broadway, she joined the legion of hopeful wannabes in Hollywood. To play the game she had been exposed to early and often as a child and for the social and screen contacts it would afford her, she had joined Lakeside.

It wasn't long after Florence, an only child, joined Lakeside that her father came out from New York to visit her. Florence's dad was a well-known golf zealot, and he played to a single-digit handicap. Her dad was Grantland Rice, the nation's number one sportswriter.

Frances took her dad out to Lakeside, and he immediately picked up on all the stories about the club's super golfer and sought a game with the man all the members called "Monty." Why, after spending the last several years of his life constantly looking over his shoulder, Monty agreed to tee it up with the country's premier sports journalist is hard to figure.

Monty held nothing back during their round. Rice was just as awestruck by Monty's game as the Lakeside members had been. In his next syndicated column, he informed the nation about the amazing golfing ability of one John Montague. He also bemoaned Montague's refusal to put his game on public display in tournament competition, stating, "The winner of the 1936 United States Amateur would be the champion only for the simple reason that John Montague is not entered." Rice then described how Montague went to great lengths to avoid being photographed and refused to discuss his life before he arrived in California.

Outed by Rice as one of the world's top golfers, the low-profile-seeking Monty was now being hunted down by the Hollywood paparazzi. They wanted a photo of the golfer who was now being called "the Mysterious Montague." Monty took evasive action, keeping an ultra-low profile and slipping out of town for a series of long stretches. And just as it appeared that the heat was about to die down, Westbrook Pegler, another popular nationally syndicated columnist, devoted a column to the amazing golfing ability of the Mysterious Montague, and the heat instantly went back to red hot.

Rice's and Pegler's columns led to what had to be one of the first major kills for the Hollywood paparazzi. They began gunning for Monty like the planes firing at King Kong on the Empire State Building. There were several occasions when Monty ran down photographers who had snapped his picture and took the film from them or smashed their cameras. He always took some of the edge off of these encounters by immediately reaching into his pocket and reimbursing the photographer for his loss. But there were just too many coming at him, and he was soon nailed on the course at Lakeside.

It took Monty several moments to locate the source of the camera clicks that had captured his image. He then raced over to the photographer and demanded the film. The photographer sheepishly ejected the film from his camera and handed it over. Monty thought he had dodged another bullet. But this photographer was pretty cagey. While Monty had been searching for the source of the clicks, he had quickly replaced the film magazine in his camera. The clicks from that camera would ultimately lead to the clicking of the teletype at the Los Angeles County Sheriff's Department.

The photographer shopped the photos, and *Time* magazine snapped them up and used them as part of a major piece titled "The Mysterious Montague." As soon as it hit the newsstands, it created an enormous amount of buzz about John Montague, and he was soon the most talked about golfer in the country. The buzz about him even stretched across the Atlantic, as the *London Times* reported that he was going to play in the British Open. Soon there was a glut of Monty stories in other publications. One of these articles, which contained the story of Monty using garden implements to put a dent in Bing Crosby's wallet, caught the eye of an Upstate New York police inspector. He thought the article might be of interest to John Lynch, a fellow inspector in a neighboring jurisdiction. So he clipped out the piece and sent it to him.

Inspector Lynch was living a role similar to the one actor Tommy Lee Jones would play over a half-century later as Lieutenant Sam Gerard in the movie *The Fugitive*. Lynch's hunt would not start at a train wreck but at the wreck of an armed robbery getaway car. In the car's trunk were a set of golf clubs and press clippings covering the athletic accomplishments of one Laverne Moore.

Mr. Moore had been a very well-known resident of Syracuse, New York, from both the sports pages and the police blotter. As a teenager, he had been heralded as an athletic prodigy and had been given the nickname "Bull." He stood 5-foot-10and weighed 220 pounds, but it was all brawn. He had tremendous hands, bulldog shoulders, and amazing foot speed for his size. Laverne excelled in all the major team sports—football, basketball, and baseball—and he had college recruiters and professional baseball scouts drooling. But it was golf where he shined the most.

Laverne's brother was a golf professional. And with a little instruction from him, combined with his enormous natural talent, the result was a golfer the likes of which the area had never seen. At the city's nine-hole course at Brunet Park, he set the course record with a 28, and on its 380-yard par-four eighth hole, he routinely placed his drive just 40 yards from the green. His big drives and low scores were just part of his game. They seemed to take a back seat to his penchant for perfecting as many trick shots as possible.

The athletic director at the University of Syracuse placed Laverne in a prep school, hoping to stimulate his academic interests and lay the foundation for a productive athletic career at his school. But the higher learning environment, or anything to do with work for that matter, did not appeal to the young man, and he dropped out of the school after just one year.

Professional baseball then took its shot at taming the Bull. He was signed first by the Braves and then later by the Yankees, but both of those opportunities fizzled out after promising starts. He also tried working as a pro at a country club, but that employment ended quickly as well.

Between and after those opportunities, Laverne kicked around Syracuse and the Adirondacks in Upstate New York. He owned a Cadillac and always seemed to have money yet had no job. His arrest for posing as a police officer and shaking down a grocer for protection money was a clear indication of the road he was headed down.

Shortly after midnight on August 7, 1930, four men robbed an Essex County roadhouse of $800, and for their escape they had paired off in two separate getaway cars. In less than forty-eight hours, Inspector Lynch and his fellow officers could account for three of the four members of the gang. One was on a morgue slab, having died from the injuries he received when he crashed his getaway car, and the other two were in custody. The fourth member of the gang, who they believed, thanks to the items discovered in the trunk of one of the getaway cars, was Laverne Moore, had given them the slip.

Lynch tracked Moore to his mother's home in Syracuse, some 200 miles away, but the officers got there just a few hours too late. When they arrived, Mrs. Moore advised them that Laverne had left town shortly after breakfast and had told her he was off to pursue a career in either baseball or golf. Initially there were some leads, but Moore's trail soon turned ice-cold, and his case eventually landed in the cold case file. The crime was approaching its seventh anniversary when the envelope containing the "Mysterious Montague" article landed on Lynch's desk.

Approximately ten days after the first contact between Inspector Lynch and the Los Angeles County authorities, Monty was cruising down a Hollywood street in his roadster when he looked over his shoulder for the last time and saw a black-and-white police car. The jig was up.

EVEN MORE HOLLYWOOD'S HUSTLER

Once at police headquarters, Monty's fingerprints were taken, and they matched the prints of Laverne Moore that had been sent by Inspector Lynch. It took the press about twenty-four hours to pick up on his arrest. But when they did, it triggered a major media frenzy. Monty seemed to be taking the situation in stride, demonstrating his golf grip for photographers from his jail cell. Meanwhile his Hollywood friends were rallying around him. They got him a lawyer and spoke to the press on his behalf.

For a while Monty and his lawyer considered fighting extradition, and his Hollywood friends put some heat on the governor of California for him to intervene, but they ultimately decided their best bet was to return to New York and face the charges. Monty was taken back to Elizabethtown, New York, the county seat of Essex County, to stand trial. He spent two nights in jail before he was arraigned and formally charged, and a trial date was set for two months from that day. Monty's bond was set at $30,000, and Bing Crosby posted the bail for his friend.

Monty retained James Noonan to head up his legal team. Noonan was a high-powered defense attorney from Albany, New York, who had recently defended mobster Dutch Schultz against federal income tax evasion charges.

When the trial got underway, the prosecution presented a very strong case. The first officers on the scene of the wrecked getaway car testified about finding golf clubs and personal effects belonging to Laverne Moore in its trunk. A witness, who was in the roadhouse at the time of the robbery, testified that the other members of the gang had called the man who appeared to be the leader "Verne." One of the two other surviving members of the gang, who had spent four years in prison for his part in the crime, took the stand and stated that Laverne Moore was the fourth member of the gang that night. He detailed how he and Moore had fled the scene in the second getaway car and then split up.

The defense's case was as weak as the prosecution's had been strong. Monty's alibi was that he had been 200 miles away in Syracuse working on his golf game at about the time the robbery took place. To support this contention, Noonan called to the stand a friend of Monty, who testified he had given him a ride home at about midnight from a local driving range. Monty's gray-haired mother then took the stand and swore that her son had gotten home around midnight on the evening in question and had gone straight to bed.

Mrs. Moore was followed to the stand by the other surviving member of the gang, a career criminal who had served five years for his part in the robbery and was now back in prison for another crime. He swore that the fourth robber was a stranger the rest of the gang had only met the day before the crime. And this man had only identified himself as "Burns," and that was the name that the victims had heard called out during the robbery. This witness's testimony ended late on a Friday afternoon, and court was adjourned for the weekend.

When the court reconvened on the following Monday for what would be the final day of the trial, Noonan spent much of the morning session reading into the court record depositions from Bing Crosby, Johnny Weissmuller, a Los Angeles priest, and ten others from the Hollywood area, all of them stating John Montague was an individual of utmost integrity and character. Then in what was considered a surprise, he called Monty to the stand to testify.

Monty did well during Noonan's questioning, but when the prosecutor began the cross-examination, his temper quickly got the best of him. He was argumentative and sneering, and he was called down by the judge for his behavior.

The prosecutor then brought out Monty's golf clubs from the wrecked getaway car and questioned him about his high-stakes golf gambling in Hollywood. Monty denied he played golf for high stakes and stated five dollars was a big bet for him. At this point the judge interrupted the prosecutor to ask Monty a question of his own. "Did you ever play Olin Dutra [1934 United States Open champion] and bet $2,500?"

"I did not," replied Monty.

Montague did confess he had been involved in rum-running with one of the robbers and had traveled with him in the area several days before the crime. But when he departed for Syracuse, he had forgotten to remove his golf clubs and other personal effects from the trunk of his car. After Monty concluded his testimony, both sides rested and then presented their closing arguments, and the case was given to the jury. Most observers thought it was a slam dunk for conviction.

Monty spent the two months between his arraignment and the start of the trial in and around Elizabethtown holding court in the lobby of his hotel, in restaurants, and in local watering holes. With his Rhett Butler charm turned up to full power, he wooed the locals with tales of his exploits: a 500-foot home run in spring training, the 58 he once shot, and the time he picked a bird off a wire with a two-wood.

One of the few times he did leave the area, the locals got to read about it in the newspapers. Monty journeyed down to Long Island to play a round with Grantland Rice. Despite not having had a club in his hands for several months, he shot a 65 on a course he had never seen before. The news about the round was picked up by a major wire service, and it received newspaper coverage across the country.

How well the public relations campaign was going was evident when Monty showed up at the courthouse for the first day of jury selection and was besieged by autograph seekers. Monty didn't let up on his public relations campaign once the proceedings started. During the weekend that the court was in recess, several members of the jury were allowed to leave the hotel to attend Mass at the local Catholic church. Shortly after they arrived, they noticed Monty was sitting in the pew beside them.

The jury deliberated for almost five hours and then returned to the courtroom and shocked everyone when they rendered a not-guilty verdict. Pandemonium broke out in the courtroom, and the judge angrily ordered it be cleared. He then admonished the jury, saying, "I am sorry to say that your verdict is not in accord with the one I think should have been rendered." He then dismissed the jury and adjourned the proceeding. Then in a scene that looked like the ultimate "Hollywood ending," two of Monty's supporters hoisted him up on their shoulders and carried him outside, where he was greeted by the cheers of a large crowd.

On its editorial page the next day, the *New York Times* weighed in on the verdict, stating, "Juries exist not only to render justice but to make mistakes occasionally."

For Monty it appeared that he was now poised to cash in on his fame and golfing ability. Bing Crosby's brother Elliot was going to be his agent, and rumors were flying about possible movie roles. Also, a series of golf instructional films were reportedly in the works.

A few days after his acquittal, Monty accepted an offer to officially take his golf game public for the first time. He agreed to team up with noted female amateur Sylva Annenberg in a match for charity against Babe Ruth and Babe Didrikson at the Fresh Meadows Country Club in New York City.

On a brisk November Sunday morning, a throng beyond the promoter's wildest expectations showed up to witness the match. The crowd's number rivaled the size of the one that had gathered to watch the final day of play at that year's United States Open. There was a slight semblance of order before the players teed off at the first hole, but as soon as the last member of the foursome hit their opening drive, the scene became one of chaos, as the large throng completely overwhelmed what limited crowd control measures had been put in place.

The spectators were standing in such close proximity to the participants that they had to be very careful not to strike them with either their backswing or their follow-through. On a par three the crowd encircled the green, and the players had to play their tee shots over their heads. The situation grew worse and worse, and the match had to be called after only nine holes, with Ruth and Babe Didrikson leading two up.

Those who had attended the event hoping to see Monty hit some incredible shots left disappointed. Monty played like a very good golfer but not a super golfer, and most people chalked it up to the conditions in which he had had to play.

A few days after that match, Monty returned to California, and soon a rumor was circulating widely through New York City that raised eyebrows: Monty and Babe Ruth had squared off in a head-to-head match before Monty left town, and Ruth had won, But Monty had left town without paying off on the match's wager. After a few weeks, Ruth, an eight handicap at that time, agreed to speak to a reporter about the match. He said it was true that he had beaten Monty in a head-to-head match five up with four to play.

Babe said that he'd had a good day and that Montague had been a little wild off the tee and that is why he had come out on top. He denied the story that Montague had left town owing him big money and then stated, "I do not play well enough to play for high stakes."

Maybe public exposure was Kryptonite to Monty because it seemed that the Ruth match was a harbinger of what was to come. Montague in Hollywood, the sequel, did not pan out as everyone had expected. The movie roles that were supposed to be in the offing never materialized, as the studio bosses steered clear of him because they were wary of the image problems he could create. The golf instructional films never got off the ground either, and his golf game remained in the non-incredible state it dropped to in the Big Apple. Montague's time on the course diminished. He played in an occasional exhibition match and made one major appearance at the United States Open in Cleveland in 1940, but his performance was hardly notable, as he posted an opening round of 80, followed by a second-round 82. He then packed his bags and headed back to California.

There was, however, a big romantic theme in the sequel. The day after he was arrested in Los Angeles, a striking brunette had arrived at police headquarters to pick up Montague's roadster from the impound lot. The same woman had been at Montague's side a good deal of the time in Elizabethtown and had sat in the first row of spectators behind the defense table during the trial. Her name was Esther Putman, and she was a wealthy Beverly Hills widow. Shortly after Montague's return to California, they were married, and Monty went from having no address to having three, as the couple divided their time between Esther's homes in Malibu, Palm Springs, and Beverly Hills.

Unfortunately for him, the good life lasted only seven years. Esther died, and Monty was never quite the same. Several real estate investments he had made went sour, and he was almost killed when his car plowed into a parked vehicle on a busy Los Angeles street in 1955. In 1970 Monty was found dead in his LA motel room. Some of his old friends from Lakeside dug into their pockets one more time for him to fund his burial. Monty had spent his last days in LA just as he had spent his first, hanging around a golf course, virtually penniless, looking for some action.

A BAG IN ONE

In the opening round of the Tournament Players Championship in 1987 in Ponte Vedra Beach, Florida, Raymond Floyd's drive at the eleventh hole was one of the most memorable shots of the event. It is unlikely it could ever be replicated, nor should any player want to do so because it cost Floyd a two-shot penalty.

Floyd, the 1986 United States Open winner, was playing in a threesome with Seve Ballesteros, the winner of two Masters and two British Opens, and Andy North, a two-time United States Open champion. The group started their round on the back nine. After playing the tenth hole, the three took their drivers to the eleventh tee, while their caddies took their bags to the approximate landing area for drives at the par-five hole.

Eddie Terrell, Floyd's caddie, took up a position well off the fairway, some 260 yards from the tee box. He laid down Floyd's bag and turned around to speak to someone in the gallery. When Floyd hit his tee shot, his ball headed toward Eddie and his bag. When the shot hit the ground, it settled into a steady roll in the direction of the bag. As if laser guided, the ball rolled into the top of it for a "bag-in-one."

Rule 19-2 of the "Rules of Golf" states: "If a competitor's ball is deflected or stopped by himself, his caddie or equipment, the competitor shall incur a penalty of two strokes." Floyd ended up with a seven on the hole.

SOME GOLF ON THE SILVER SCREEN

On the practice tee in the run-up to a PGA event in 2021, there was a very strange sight. Tiger Woods, Dustin Johnson, Rory McIlroy, Collin Morikawa, Matthew Wolff, and Tommy Fleetwood were wearing hockey jerseys. The group was paying tribute to the twenty-fifth anniversary of the film *Happy Gilmore*.

The film stars Adam Sandler as Happy Gilmore. Happy is an unsuccessful hockey player who turns to golf. He enters professional golf and makes a splash on tour using a unique swing, in which he gets a running start before hitting his shot.

The group of PGA stars were all going to take a shot at executing Happy's swing. All but one were guilty of being tentative in their execution, essentially doing a slow jog up to the ball. The one player who was on target with Happy's method was Rory McIlroy, who approached the shot at full-bore. While his style was an A+, his results were not. His shots were an assortment of bad strikes and near misses.

One of the most talked about parts of the film is the fight between Happy Gilmore and Bob Barker, the longtime host of *The Price Is Right*.

The two are paired together as partners in a tournament, and throughout their round, Happy's play is not up to par. This leads to words being exchanged between the two, which ultimately leads to a fight. To everyone's surprise, the much older Barker wins the bout.

Ed McMahon, Johnny Carson's longtime sidekick, was originally hired to do Barker's role. He backed out because the script called for his character to lose the fight with Happy. He was also turned off by the script's crude humor. Barker was selected as a replacement because Chuck Norris was Barker's neighbor and had taught him karate. The script was later changed to make Barker the winner of the fight.

Follow the Sun is a 1951 biographical film of the life of Ben Hogan. It follows how, through his diligence and tenacity, he reaches the top ranks of golf and makes a gigantic comeback after being mangled in a traffic accident. It stars Glenn Ford as Hogan and Anne Baxter as his wife.

Ford was not a golfer, so Ben Hogan stepped in to be his instructor. When their instructional sessions were completed, Hogan gave Ford the set of clubs he had used to win the U.S. Open. Ford practiced golf for a month, four hours per day, before production began. He became a solid player, but Ford never played golf again after shooting was completed.

A close-up near the end of the movie shows Glenn Ford about to tee off at the Los Angeles Open. When the scene cuts to a wide shot and the tee shot is played, the golfer shown is Ben Hogan himself.

In the 2004 film *The Aviator*, Howard Hughes was played by Leonardo DiCaprio, who, like Glenn Ford, was not a golfer. To prepare him for the golf scenes in the film, Jim Venetos, a well-known golf instructor, was engaged to give DiCaprio lessons. Because of time constraints, he had time for just three fifteen-minute sessions with DiCaprio.

The first session took place in the backyard of DiCaprio's home. After receiving some basic instructions, DiCaprio took his first swing. Using a nine-iron, he unleashed a 150-yard shot with a slight draw. The ball struck a neighboring house. Venetos had a look of concern on his face after the ball impacted the house. DiCaprio smiled at him and said, "Don't worry, I own that house too."

DiCaprio then took his second swing. This one did not come off as well. He whiffed it. On-screen, DiCaprio and Cate Blanchett, who played

Katharine Hepburn and who was also given instruction by Venetos, handled their golf scenes in good form.

Great actors are not usually accomplished athletes, but Katharine Hepburn was an exception. She was a talented golfer. She was also one of the best tennis players in Hollywood. Hepburn showcased her prowess in both games in the 1952 film *Pat and Mike* costarring Spencer Tracy.

In the film Hepburn portrays Pat Pemberton, a brilliant golf and tennis player. Women's golf and tennis championships are within her reach; however, she gets flustered when her domineering fiancé, played by Aldo Ray, is around. He wants her to give up her goals and marry him, but Pat does not give up on herself that easily. She enlists the help of Mike Conovan (Spencer Tracy), a slightly shady sports promoter. Together they face mobsters, a jealous boxer, and a growing mutual attraction. In one of Hepburn's golf matches, she loses to one of the great female golfers of all time, Babe Didrikson Zaharias, who plays herself in the film.

ESPN labeled *Caddyshack* as perhaps the funniest sports movie ever made. The 1980 release about the wild characters of the Bushwood Country Club became an almost cult classic. Harold Ramis made his directorial debut with this film. His biggest complaint was that no one in the film except for Bill Murray, who played Carl Spackler, could swing his or her golf club properly.

Murray improvised the film's iconic "Cinderella story" sequence from two lines of stage direction. Director Ramis simply asked Murray to imagine himself announcing his own fantasy sports moment. Murray asked for four rows of chrysanthemums to do the scene.

Murray smashed each of the chrysanthemums with an eight-iron. As he was in the process of smashing the last one and following its imaginary flight, he uttered these lines: "Cinderella story. Outta nowhere. A former greenskeeper, now, about to become the Masters champion. [*He smashes the chrysanthemum.*] It looks like a mirac—It's in the hole! It's in the hole! It's in the hole!"

In a survey conducted by the American Film Institute, those lines ranked 92 out of 100 in the top movie quotations of all time.

A big hill was built from scratch for the climactic eighteenth-hole scene when Carl Spackler tries to blow up the gopher that has plagued him throughout the film. The pyrotechnic people used too many explosives, and the result was quite a blast. The course where the film was shot was on one of the main flight paths into the Fort Lauderdale International Airport. When the blast was detonated, the pilot of a commercial flight on its final approach reported to Air Traffic Control that a plane had crashed.

In *Tin Cup* Kevin Costner portrays a washed-up golf pro working at a driving range who tries to qualify for the U.S. Open to win the heart of his successful rival's girlfriend. Many of the golf shots by Kevin Costner's character (Roy McAvoy) were actual shots by Costner himself. He'd had some exposure to golf before taking the part and worked hard before shooting began to develop a solid game.

Don Johnson contends he got the part of Roy McAvoy's rival (David Sims) because he was the only actor in Hollywood who could genuinely play golf. He was a ten handicap when filming started. But thanks to all the instruction from the golf pros and golf instructors involved with the film, when shooting was over, he was a three.

The scene at the end of the movie in which Roy keeps hitting shots into a lake again and again is based on an actual event. Gary McCord plays the television commentator covering Roy's play of the hole. McCord was an actual CBS golf commentator and a former player on the PGA Tour. In a 1987 tournament, McCord had a shot similar to Kevin Costner's. He needed a birdie to win and went for it. He hit the water over and over again and finally made the shot, but it cost him fifteen strokes. In the movie Costner gets it in twelve. The scene in which Roy wins a bar bet by hitting a golf ball at a pelican also was based on a real-life incident from McCord's career.

Before filming at the Tubac Golf Resort began in the Arizona desert, there was not a lake on the course. For the big scene when Roy repeatedly tries to hit his ball over the water, a lake had to be made. The crew named it "Tin Cup Lake."

Cheech Marin disliked golf when he took the part of Roy's friend and caddie. After filming, he became an avid golfer.

THE PRESIDENT'S CADDIE

After winning the presidential election in November 1908, William Howard Taft took two monthlong golf vacations before his inauguration, which at that time took place in March instead of January. His first began a few days after his election, and it was at Hot Springs, Virginia, and the second was at Augusta, Georgia. Hot Springs was a popular golf retreat for the well-to-do; both Andrew Carnegie and John D. Rockefeller spent considerable time on its course. When these gentlemen played there, they both used the services of a caddie who was considered the resort course's best. He was a young man named Elmer Loving.

Loving had just a year or two of schooling, and his income from caddying helped support his family. He had been caddying since the age of ten, and now in his late teens, he had worked on his own game whenever he could and had developed into a top-flight player. When President-Elect Taft arrived, naturally Elmer was given the assignment as his caddie. Taft was immediately struck by his young caddie's character, and a strong bond developed between the two. As Taft's stay was ending, he decided he would ask Loving to become a member of his White House team.

The president-elect had high hopes for Elmer's future. The plan was he would work at the White House as Taft's personal messenger during the day. In the evenings Elmer would attend night school with the goal of ultimately making it to the University of Virginia in Charlottesville to study law.

Elmer would eventually make it to Charlottesville, but it was not as a student but as a golf professional. He was in Washington DC for a couple of years, first at the White House and then President Taft farmed him out to the postmaster general, who happened to be taking up golf at the time. In between his messenger duties and school, Loving found time to set course records at several courses in the DC area, Columbia Country Club and Bannockburn in Chevy Chase among them.

Loving decided that being a golf professional was his true calling and quit after two years in Washington. One of his first stops was the golf professional post at the newly opened Arcola Country Club in Paramus, New Jersey. He played in the 1913 U.S. Open at Brookline won by Francis Ouimet and finished in eleventh place. At the U.S. Open at Baltusrol in 1915, he finished thirty-second.

Loving eventually landed in Charlottesville and served many years as the head professional at the Charlottesville Country Club.

JOHN F. KENNEDY

The Hit-and-Run Golfer

It was cloudy and damp, and the temperature was hovering in the low forties on February 21, 1961, in Washington DC when, shortly after noon, President Kennedy's limo eased out the White House gate onto Pennsylvania Avenue. Several members of the White House press corps had observed the limo's departure. They immediately sought out JFK's assistant press secretary, Andrew Hatcher, who was handling the press briefings that afternoon and quizzed him on where the president had gone. Hatcher replied that all he knew was that the president had gone someplace with Senator George Smathers of New Jersey.

Hatcher's response piqued the interest of the entire press corps, and they kept pressing for an answer about the president's whereabouts. An hour later Hatcher returned to the press room. He apologized for not having been more forthcoming earlier about JFK's whereabouts, but he had not been authorized to say anything. He had now been cleared to report the president's location, announcing that JFK was at the Chevy Chase Country Club, playing golf with Senator Smathers and Senator Stuart Symington of Missouri.

One could understand why Kennedy's staff was a little skittish about revealing JFK's whereabouts. As the 1960 presidential campaign had heated up between Kennedy and Eisenhower's vice president, Richard Nixon, Kennedy and his running mate, Lyndon Johnson, had worked "the golf card" against Nixon.

Johnson's campaign speeches below the Mason-Dixon Line almost always included this line: "The only thing the Republicans have used the South for over the last eight years was a golf course to tee off from." Kennedy was a little subtler, not wishing to attack Eisenhower's frequent golf playing directly because of Eisenhower's high popularity. He often modified a line from T. S. Eliot's poem "Choruses from 'The Rock'" when he addressed crowds during campaign stops:

And the wind shall say: "Here were decent people:
Their only monument the asphalt road
And a thousand lost golf balls."

Concerns about how the Democrats were using golf as a campaign issue against Nixon resulted in Eisenhower turning down a very prestigious golf honor from the home of golf, the Royal and Ancient Club of St. Andrews. Just as the campaign was heating up, the R&A informally contacted Eisenhower through an intermediary asking if he would look with favor on being nominated to serve as their captain.

The captain's position was created in the mid-1860s. The appointment begins in late September, and its term is twelve months. At that time only one American had ever served in the post, Francis Ouimet, whose win in the U.S. Open at Brookline in 1913 is credited with bringing golf into America's mainstream.

The annual installation of the captain is held with much fanfare in a ceremony during which he hits a drive from the first tee at the Old Course to begin his term during the R&A membership's fall meeting. The duties of the post are to essentially serve as an ambassador for the game and to be the figurehead of the R&A's worldwide membership.

Eisenhower was honored to have been asked to serve. But he sent word back that he would have to decline. He was uncomfortable in accepting the post in the midst of a presidential election for fear it would end up being fodder in the political arena.

The Kennedy-Johnson campaign's jabs at golf made the fact that JFK was a golfer a hush-hush item. He did get in a few rounds during the campaign. The members of the press covering his campaign were not permitted to cover his golf, and photographers were requested not to take pictures. During one of these hush-hush golf outings at Monterey, California, Kennedy just missed making a hole in one.

In an interview soon after the election, Walter Hall, Kennedy's pro at the Hyannis Port, Massachusetts, club where he learned the game, described JFK as a "hit-and-run golfer" and stated he had been at the club for sixteen years and had never seen him play a full round of eighteen holes. He would play seven or eight holes and zoom; he was off to other things.

Hall's assessment of JFK's golf was that he could easily shoot in the '70s if he altered his approach to the game. Hall had made Kennedy's clubs. The set was lighter in weight than normal and included a two-wood JFK preferred to use off the tee. His typical drives with that club traveled from 225 to 250 yards.

Christopher Dunphy was the president of the famous Seminole Golf Club, which was near the Kennedy family's winter vacation home near Palm Beach, Florida. He played a number of times with JFK there and described him as one of the most relaxed and composed golfers he had ever seen.

Immediately after his election, Kennedy took a page out of Taft's, Harding's, and Eisenhower's playbook and went on a golfing binge before his inauguration. He spent a good bit of December in Florida, playing almost every day. Notables who spent some time with the president-elect on the course were his brother Robert, his vice president–elect, Lyndon Johnson, and a man who had voted for Richard Nixon in the election, the Reverend Billy Graham.

Over Eisenhower's two terms in office, the criticism by the press over the amount of time he spent playing golf had built up steadily. The *New York Times* on December 28, 1960, decided that too much had been made of Eisenhower's golf by the critics and the jesters and voiced the hope that President-Elect Kennedy would not be criticized for teeing it up in an editorial:

> *There have been a lot of jokes about Presidential Golf—some good, some bad. In a drab world we hesitate to say there could ever be too many jokes, but it is just possible that jokes about the President playing golf are in oversupply. We make unusual demands, indeed cruel demands that they sit incessantly in sackcloth studying official documents. The critics and jesters would lose their sport if the President took his recreation indoors as in a game of poker, an evening with a whodunit, previewing a movie or watching a western on television. Mr. Kennedy has been playing golf almost daily in Florida. He apparently enjoys the game. He may not play so well as to suggest a misspent youth, but if he plays only on vacation he will certainly play worse rather than better when he finishes his term in office. This is nothing to worry about. But the nation might well worry its conscience over whether it has been having so much uncharitable fun with Presidential golf that it has made a trip around the course a political liability too great for a President to bear. That would be absurd. Mr. Kennedy cannot afford to let other people dictate how he takes his exercise.*

For his Easter vacation in 1961, JFK headed back to Palm Beach. Soon after his arrival, he teed it up with his father, Joseph Kennedy, and his brothers-in-law Stephen Smith and actor Peter Lawford. On a tee shot, JFK hit a severe hook that struck a Secret Service agent who was positioned off the fairway's left side. The agent was taken to the hospital to be checked out and returned to his duties later that afternoon. Republicans who had been ravaged by Democrats for Eisenhower's golf were quick to point out that this trip to the course by JFK put him one trip to the course ahead of Eisenhower at the same time in his presidency.

Two weeks later JFK was spending the weekend at the northern Virginia farm he was using as a retreat. On Sunday morning he was playing golf with his sister, Jean, and her husband, Stephen Smith, but his mind was very much on Cuba. He was scheduled to give, by noon that day, the final go-ahead for the Bay of Pigs invasion. A force of Cuban exiles trained and supplied by the United States was going to land on Cuba's south coast in an attempt to overthrow the Communist regime of Fidel Castro. JFK struggled with whether to go through with it. At two in the afternoon, two hours after the time he said he would give the go or no-go command, he called his secretary of state, who was his conduit for the operation, and gave him the go-ahead. Shortly after giving the order, he went outside with his two-wood and hit golf ball after golf ball into an adjoining cornfield.

The operation was a disaster, with most of the invasion force captured or killed. As a debacle, it was a ten on a ten scale. A week later Kennedy asked Eisenhower to meet with him at Camp David to go over the ill-fated operation. The two went for a long private walk on the grounds. As they were parting ways after their meeting, JFK suggested they should get together for a game of golf soon.

A few weeks later, however, Kennedy's trips to the course came to an almost complete halt when he seriously aggravated a back problem while participating in a tree planting ceremony in Ottawa, Canada. As a result, his outdoor activities from that point were primarily restricted to boating.

ONE OF THE GAME OF GOLF'S MOST STAUNCH TRADITIONALISTS MAKES THE SWITCH

When it comes to golf, it is unlikely that there is anybody in the game who is more of a traditionalist than Jack Nicklaus. But in 1988, at the Doral Open in Miami, he let go of tradition, at least as it pertained to the type of driver he used. After winning eighty-nine professional tournaments with a driver made from persimmon, Jack made the switch to metal, joining the now over 50 percent of PGA Tour players who had already made the switch.

Metal woods were first introduced in 1979 by TaylorMade Golf. The transition to the club by tour players was slow but steady. The first player to win a tournament with a metal driver was Jim Simons in 1982, at the Bing Crosby National Pro-Am at Pebble Beach. Lee Trevino became the first player to win a major title using a metal wood when he captured the PGA Championship in 1984, which gave the movement from wood to metal even more momentum.

Jack's first outing with metal was impressive. In strong winds he traveled around the treacherous Blue Monster course at Doral with precision, hitting thirteen of fourteen fairways. On the one he missed, it was only by a few feet. He shot a four-under sixty-eight, which left him just one stroke out of the lead.

With his new driver, Jack stayed in the top five through round 3. He slipped in the final round, when he shot a 3 over 75, and he finished in twenty-fourth place.

A CADDIE NAMED SHIRLEY

On June 5, 1998, the *Washington Post* ran the last column by its legendary sportswriter Shirley Povich. Shirley had died the night before from a heart condition at age ninety-two. His long association with the *Washington Post* had been triggered by Shirley's days as a caddie in his hometown of Bar Harbor, Maine, at the Kebo Valley Golf Club.

At his birth his parents chose the name Shirley as it was a very popular name for males in their area. But during his long career, it sometimes caused a problem for Shirley and made him the target of ribbing.

Shirley's big break came at a young age, when he had the good fortune to carry the golf bag one day for a golf fanatic from Washington DC. His name was Ned McLean, and he was the owner of the *Washington Post*. Shirley turned in an excellent caddie performance that day, earning a two-dollar tip plus his fee for the round of eighty-five cents. Shirley's services were retained for the rest of Mr. McLean's lengthy stay and the following summer as well.

In 1922, Povich's second year caddying for McLean, the publisher asked him what he planned to do after graduating from high school. Povich told him he'd probably go to the University of Maine, where admission was virtually assured to any state resident and, more important, tuition was cheap. "Then I learned of Mr. McLean's plans for me," Povich wrote in his autobiography. "'Next Monday, my private [railroad] car is leaving for Washington, and I want you to come with me,'" McLean told me. "'You can go to my college and work on my newspaper in Washington.' His college, I learned, was Georgetown University."

Shirley, then seventeen, did not accept McLean's offer that day. But eventually, he did find his way to Washington DC and to McLean's front door. In short order he was caddying for the newspaper owner on weekends on McLean's private nine-hole course at his residence. One of the players in McLean's regular weekend group was the president of the United States, Warren G. Harding. During the week Shirley was working as a copyboy at the *Post*. He wasn't a copyboy for long, though—he became a sports reporter and was soon named the *Post*'s sports editor in 1926, at the age of twenty-one.

Shirley became one of the nation's most respected sports journalists. His tenure as the *Post*'s sports editor lasted until his retirement forty-seven years later, in 1973. In retirement he continued to write columns for the *Post* until his death.

Shirley never forgot the game that led to his long and outstanding career. He was a longtime member of the Woodmont Country Club in Rockville, Maryland, and at his game's peak, he played to a six handicap. One of Shirley's favorite assignments was covering the Masters.

THE MIGHTY MO

At the 2014 Ricoh Women's British Open at the Royal Birkdale Golf Club in Southport, England, Mo Martin was the type of feel-good story that often takes place at a major championship when an unheralded golfer takes center stage in the early going only to fade in the later rounds.

Mo was the feel-good story of feel-good stories. She grew up with modest means in Altadena, California, and she stood only 5-foot-2. Her father built a cage in their driveway for her to practice hitting balls. He nicknamed her the "Mighty Mo" after the navy battleship *Missouri* that had punished the Japanese in the closing stages of World War II and on whose deck the Japanese had formally surrendered.

The trek to the LPGA Tour for Mo would be quite the uphill climb. She was a walk-on on the UCLA golf team and toiled for six long seasons on the minor league Symetra Tour. Plenty of players have given up after a few years of the nomadic, penny-watching existence of the Symetra Tour but not her.

Mo was at the ripe old age of twenty-nine when she finally made it to the LPGA Tour. She didn't have a coach. She didn't have an agent, and she didn't have any sponsors. In her sixty-four starts on tour, she had only one top-ten finish, and that one qualified her for the Ricoh British Open.

Mo was the mega-surprise leader after thirty-six holes, leading by three strokes after consecutive rounds of 69, but it appeared her chances were doused in the third round, when she carded a 77. This left her in a seven-way tie for seventh place at one under par.

When her final round ended, Mo was still at one under par, but she had the lead thanks to her remarkable eagle at the par-five eighteenth hole. Mo's average driving distance on tour was in the bottom third, at 233 yards. After her drive on eighteen, she was 240 yards from the flag. With the wind at her back, she decided to go for it.

Mo swung her three-wood with all she had and made good contact, but the shot fell some thirty yards short of the green. She thought she was going to end up short, but her ball kept rolling. When it reached the putting surface, it still had plenty of steam. Mo was concerned it would roll off the back of the green. And that was exactly where it was heading until something got in its way—the flagstick. Her ball struck the flagstick and caromed off to the right. It came to rest six feet from the cup, and Mo did a little dance.

On the green Mo lined up her eagle putt. She got over the putt and then backed off. She lined it up again and rolled it in. The eagle was her first of the 2014 season, and it gave her the clubhouse lead.

Mo finished almost an hour before the six golfers who were ahead of her when the day started. They were all struggling. When it was over, Mo was the winner, edging out Shanshan Feng and Suzann Pettersen by one stroke. She received a champagne shower from her friends on tour and a check for $474,575.

THE UNITED STATES' FIRST OLYMPIC GOLFERS

The first time golf was part of the games was in Paris in 1900. An American, Charles Sands—the same Charles Sands who had lost to Charles Macdonald in the first United States Amateur in 1895 and won a big-money golf match soon after—won the gold medal.

Golf was a very late addition to the 1900 games. On the men's side, Sands had gone to the Paris games as a member of the American tennis team. He stepped up to represent the United States in the golf event along with Frederick Taylor, a member of the United States' fencing team, and Albert Lambert, a prominent St. Louis businessman, who was in Paris for work. In 1889, upon his father's death, Lambert had taken over the reins of his father's company, the Lambert Pharmacal Company (later Lambert Pharmaceuticals). The company was the license holder and marketer of a product created as a surgical antiseptic but had found its true calling as a mouthwash: Listerine.

The rest of the twelve-man field was composed of four golfers each from France and Great Britain and one from Greece. It was a thirty-six-hole stroke play event. Sands was the winner, shooting rounds of 82 and

85, for a 167 total. Walter Rutherford of Scotland took second place, with a score of 168. Frederick Taylor finished in fourth place, and Lambert came in eighth.

Upon his return to St. Louis, Lambert took the lead in setting up the golf event there for the 1904 Olympics. The format for the event was changed from medal play to match play. Lambert was again a participant, making it to the quarterfinals before losing to the eventual winner, Canadian George Lyon, five and four.

On a trip to Paris after the 1904 Olympics, Lambert became interested in hot-air ballooning. From ballooning he advanced to airplanes, taking flight lessons from, and also purchasing a plane from, Orville Wright. Lambert became a leading proponent of aviation and its future. The plane Charles Lindbergh flew on the first solo flight across the Atlantic was named the *Spirit of St. Louis* in honor of a group of his supporters in St. Louis led by Lambert, who had paid for the aircraft.

Also in the 1900 games, there was a golf event for women, and it had to be one of the oddest Olympic competitions of all time. Some in the field would go to their graves not knowing they had participated in an Olympic event.

Tennis and golf events had been scheduled for the women, but these events were thought to be sports demonstrations, not Olympic events. It was not until well after the 1900 games had concluded that the International Olympic Committee sanctioned these competitions as actual Olympic events.

Margret Ives Abbott was an American student studying in Paris, and she won the nine-hole event with a score of 47. There were nine other golfers in the field, four others from the United States and five from France. The other Americans in the field finished second, third, fifth, and seventh.

Abbott went on to become a newspaperwoman and a novelist. She married writer, author, and humorist Peter Finley Dunne, and they had four children. She died in 1955.

In the run-up to the 1996 Olympics in Atlanta, sports historian Paula Welch, a professor at the University of Florida, was conducting research on the event in 1900 and contacted Abbott's surviving children. They were unaware that their mother had been an Olympic champion. She had talked about the victory in Paris with her family, describing it as just another tournament.

Margaret's mother was visiting her in Paris at the time of the Olympics, and she also teed it up in the event. She was the seventh-place finisher. Margaret's father was the book reviewer for the *Chicago Tribune*. Both Margaret and her mother's home course was Charles B. Macdonald's Chicago Country Club.

WILL ROGERS'S DISDAIN FOR GOLF

From the early 1920s through the mid-1930s, Will Rogers's folksy commentary in his newspaper column captured the hearts of rank-and-file Americans across the breadth of the country. The same could not be said for the game of golf. Since gaining a foothold in the northeastern United States in the late 1880s, the game had struggled to catch on across most of the rest of the country.

Golf was played primarily at country clubs, and as one would expect, it took on the look of a highbrow activity for the rich, who golfed and yachted as they summered. This impression was given tremendous reinforcement by the fact that two of the country's most talked about golf zealots were Andrew Carnegie and John D. Rockefeller, the country's two richest citizens.

Golf's deep connection to the nation's upper crust resulted in most of the country's rank and file looking at the game with contempt. This contempt was fueled by the stance on the game taken by one of the most popular United States presidents of all time: Theodore Roosevelt.

Built like a bull, Roosevelt was the quintessential man's man. While president, he hunted. He boxed. He chopped down trees. On more than one occasion, he took winter swims across the Potomac, threading his way through chunks of floating ice. Roosevelt let it be known widely and often that he viewed golf with contempt. He called it a game for dudes and snobs.

After Roosevelt's passing, in 1919, Will Rogers took point for the anti-golf crowd, drawing huge laughs about the game in his stage act and writing. Some of his more notable barbs were:

I guess there is nothing that will get your mind off everything like golf. I have never been depressed enough to take up the game, but they say you get so sore at yourself you forget to hate your enemies. Long ago when men cursed and beat the ground with sticks, it was called witchcraft. Today it's called golf.

War is just like golf. Once a fellow takes it up he won't let nothing interfere with it.

The anti-golf sentiment was potent enough that it spilled over into the 1920 United States presidential election in a substantial way. During the Republican convention in Chicago, a deal was cut by the party's bosses in the wee hours of the morning in a smoke-filled hotel room that gave the party's 1920 nomination for president to Warren G. Harding, a United States senator from Marion, Ohio.

Harding's team decided that for the general election, they would utilize a front porch campaign. Instead of barnstorming the country, their candidate would remain close to or at his Marion home and let supporters and the press come to him. Presidents Garfield, Harrison, and McKinley had made it to the White House using this strategy.

This homey approach was augmented by a well-orchestrated use of print media and a thorough stroking of the newsreel distributors. Newsreels were shown in movie houses before the main feature. They were akin to today's nightly news broadcasts.

At no time is the pulse of the American people more closely monitored than in a presidential election year. In the very early days of the Harding campaign, Republican Party leaders were panic-stricken by the public's reaction to footage in one of the first newsreels that featured their candidate. It showed Harding, adorned in fancy knickers, teeing off and putting at a golf course near his home.

As soon as the golf newsreel footage began to roll in movie houses around the country, the Harding campaign was inundated with negative reactions to it. One United States senator who was backing Harding fueled the campaign's mounting dismay. He stated that he had been in a packed theater where the newsreel was shown and reported that there was not one applauding set of hands in the entire place.

It was clear to the Harding team that they had ingested a huge dose of political poison, and they were in desperate need of an antidote to get their campaign back on track. They hatched a plan involving baseball that would show the country their man was as mainstream America as they get.

As the season moved into late August, the Chicago Cubs were on their way to another lackluster finish in the National League pennant race. But they were about to play a big role in another race—the race for the White House. Sticking to their front porch strategy, the Harding campaign planned to bring the Cubs to Marion on one of their off days for an exhibition game and use the contest as a showcase for their candidate. This plan was easy to implement because the owner of the Cubs was a Harding backer.

In the game the Cubs took on a team of locals, and a crowd of seven thousand showed up at the rickety Marion ballpark. The campaign sent out press releases a few days before the game about Harding's love for baseball. The releases chronicled Harding's playing days as a barehanded first baseman in his youth and detailed how he was once a major stockholder in a professional team in the Ohio State League.

Harding arrived at the game with the newsreel cameras rolling and received a rousing welcome from the crowd. He then warmed up the Cubs starting pitcher, future Hall of Famer Grover Cleveland Alexander. After the warm-up session, Harding threw out the first pitch and then whooped it up in the stands for the benefit of the cameras the rest of the afternoon.

The Cubs won 3–1, but Harding was the real winner. When the game's newsreel footage reached the movie houses, the favorable reaction it received more than canceled out Harding's golfing blunder. He won the election, handily defeating his Democratic opponent, James M. Cox.

Once in the Oval Office, Harding's frequent golfing and the criticism he received about it would dog him. By the second year of his presidency, it was a public relations nightmare and about to worsen because Will Rogers rolled into DC with his comedy show for an extended run of performances.

When Will arrived, he was extended an invitation to the White House to meet President Harding. His visit was cordial and friendly, and Harding expressed an interest in seeing Will's show.

In one sketch in his show, Will played a member of Harding's cabinet who received a phone call from him and then said: "You lost by two holes, Mr. President? Well, you can't expect to win every day." The joke and other golf gibes Will made at Harding were quickly passed around Washington DC. After just a few shows, one of Harding's aides went to see Will and asked that he not do so many golf jokes about the president because the newspapers were making too much of it.

Although he was surprised at the request, Rogers agreed to it and eliminated several golf jokes from his act. A couple of days later, it was announced that Harding was going out to the theater. Rogers took this to mean he was coming to see his show since the only other show in town was way below the caliber of his. But when the curtain rose, Harding was nowhere to be seen. He had gone to the other show.

Will's trademark line was "I never met a man I didn't like." It appeared Harding had come close to making Will modify that line. Rogers was uncharacteristically miffed. The following night he turned the comedic heat back up on Harding, putting the previous jokes about his golf back in his routine, plus adding more.

Will also added several jokes that were not about golf. One turned out to be quite prophetic. There had been a fire that had recently damaged the Treasury Department building. Will used the fire as a jab at Harding. He quipped: "The fire started on the roof and burned down to where the money was supposed to be and there it stopped. The Harding administration had beat the fire to it."

It was soon after Will's show left Washington DC that the biggest and most sensational scandal to hit American politics to that point broke: Teapot Dome. It involved the bribery of members of the Harding administration by oil companies for drilling rights on government property in Wyoming and California. Harding died unexpectedly a year later. Many believe it was the stress from the scandal that caused his death.

SAM SNEAD TAKES A COUPLE OF SWINGS AT WRIGLEY FIELD

In March 1939, during the PGA Tour's Florida swing, Sam Snead had already collected fifteen of his seventy-five tour victories. He had been a standout baseball player in high school and had always thought he had major league potential written all over him. Fred Corcoran, Sam's business manager, arranged with Boston Red Sox manager, Joe Cronin, for twenty-seven-year-old Sam to take batting practice with the club at their spring training site. After Sam finished what he considered a very impressive hitting display, he turned to Cronin and asked him what he thought of his performance.

Cronin, a member of baseball's Hall of Fame, with a lifetime batting average of .301 over nineteen seasons in the majors, bluntly stated he wasn't impressed. Recalling that day in an interview years later, Corcoran stated that Cronin's assessment stung Sam, producing one of the rare times he saw the great golfer miffed.

Twelve years later, in 1951, Sam was given an opportunity by the Chicago Cubs to step up to home plate at Wrigley Field, not with a bat in his hands but with a golf club. As part of the Cubs' Opening Day ceremony before their game with Cincinnati, Sam was asked to settle a long-standing argument on whether a golf ball could be hit from home plate over Wrigley Field's huge towering scoreboard mounted above the centerfield bleachers.

With a four-iron in hand, Sam made a few waggles and then let it rip. Although well struck, the shot came up just a tad short. The crowd let out a huge collective groan as the ball struck near the top of the scoreboard and caromed down into the centerfield seats.

Sam dropped back two clubs, replacing the four-iron with a two-iron, and sent a second attempt sailing over the gigantic board with plenty of room to spare, producing a roar from the Wrigley Field crowd on par with the reaction afforded a Cub batter who had delivered a grand slam.

A FORMER ARTILLERY OFFICER UNLEASHES A BIRDIE BARRAGE

Buddy Allin, a U.S. Army veteran who had been an artillery officer in Vietnam, concluded a four-day birdie barrage at the Royal Pinar Country Club near Orlando to win the 1973 Florida Citrus Open by eight strokes.

Allin grabbed the lead in the first round with a 66 and never relinquished it, shooting 65 in the second and 67 in rounds 3 and 4, to coast home eight strokes ahead of runner-up Charlie Coody. Cheering the loudest for Buddy in the gallery as he approached the home green in the final round were a captain, a major, and a colonel, all three former prisoners of war.

In 1969 Allin turned pro and qualified for the PGA Tour on his first attempt, citing the fact that golf was "no big deal" compared to war. His previous win on tour was at the Greater Greensboro Open in 1971, and it came the hard way. Buddy had to play his way into the field in the Monday qualifier and then win a three-way playoff with Dave Eichelberger and Rod Funseth. Over the remainder of his career, he would record three more PGA Tour wins.

The 5-foot-8, 140-pound Buddy was a teammate of Johnny Miller on the Brigham Young University golf team. After college he enlisted in the army and volunteered for Vietnam, where he served for eighteen months. Though Buddy never talked much about the war, he was awarded a handful of medals, including two Purple Hearts and two Bronze Stars (one with a *V* for "valor").

Buddy died in 2007 from cancer at age sixty-two. He had struggled with cancer for many years. It is suspected his cancer could have been attributable to exposure in Vietnam to Agent Orange, the defoliant used to destroy the lush jungle the enemy used for cover.

A RECORD-SETTING FINAL-ROUND COMEBACK

In the opening week of March 1994, Jay Sigel pulled off the biggest final-round comeback in American professional golf history in the PGA Senior Tour's GTE Western Classic in Ojai, California. He stormed from ten shots down on the event's last day to tie the leader, Jim Colbert. Six playoff holes later, Sigel rolled in a four-foot birdie putt to record his first win as a professional.

Sigel had long been one of the country's top amateurs. His top victories were back-to-back titles in the United States Amateur in 1982 and 1983 and the British Amateur crown in 1979. Upon reaching his fiftieth birthday, he had recently turned professional and joined the PGA Tour's Senior Tour.

Lee Trevino had initially talked Sigel out of entering the GTE Western Classic. Trevino believed the layout of the course would not fit Sigel's game. But he reconsidered when another big name on the Senior Tour, Dave Stockton, encouraged him to enter.

In his closing round, Jay shot a blistering 62 to break the course record. His ten-shot comeback eclipsed the old record of seven on both the Senior

Tour and the regular PGA Tour. Jim Colbert had entered the final round of the fifty-four-hole event well in command, at fourteen under par, but he had an off day. Still, at the final hole, he could have pulled it out with a four-foot birdie putt, but his effort slid off to the right of the cup.

One of the key moments in Jay's development as a top-notch golfer came with the help of a golf professional named Palmer. Not Arnold but Arnold's dad, Deacon. Jay was having trouble with a hook, so his father made a call to Latrobe, Pennsylvania, and made Jay an appointment for a lesson from Deacon. Father and son drove down very early one morning from their home near Philadelphia. It was worth the trip. After a four-hour session with Deacon, the hook was gone.

PRESIDENT TRUMP HONORS BABE

In 2020 President Donald J. Trump awarded the Presidential Medal of Freedom posthumously to Mildred Ella "Babe" Didrikson Zaharias. This prestigious award is the nation's highest civilian honor, which is awarded by the president to individuals who have made especially meritorious contributions to the security or national interests of the United States, to world peace, or to cultural or other significant public or private endeavors.

Babe grew up in poverty in Beaumont, Texas. She quickly became an athletic Renaissance woman. As a youth, she hit five home runs in a single baseball game and was nicknamed "Babe" after Babe Ruth. It was a name that she carried for the rest of her life. In high school Babe competed in every sport offered. She bowled a 200 average, came close to breaking world records in swimming, and won all-city and all-state awards in basketball. She could also type eighty-six words a minute.

After high school she pitched in exhibition games for major league teams and was a stand-out softball player. At the 1932 Los Angeles Olympics, Babe sprinted to a gold medal in the eighty-meter hurdles, threw the javelin for a second gold, and took silver in the high jump.

Days after competing in the LA Olympics, Babe turned to golf. She had had some exposure to the game, but this was her coming-out moment, at LA's Brentwood Country Club, to play in a foursome with the nation's top sportswriter, Grantland Rice. Wearing golf shoes she had borrowed from Brentwood's professional, Olin Dutra, who would win the 1934 United States Open, she hit drives ranging from 220 yards to 240.

Over the course of her golf career, she won ten major championships and eighty-two pro and amateur golf tournaments. She helped found the LPGA and became the first woman to play against men in a PGA Tour event. Babe was voted Female Athlete of the Year six times by the Associated Press.

In 1953 she was diagnosed with colon cancer and underwent surgery. The doctors said she would never play professional golf again. A year after her surgery, Babe won the women's U.S. Open by a record twelve shots.

There was a recurrence of her cancer in 1955, which resulted in her death in September 1956, at the age of forty-five.

FRIDAY THE THIRTEENTH

Seven years after their loss to Francis Ouimet in a playoff at the 1913 U.S. Open at the Country Club at Brookline, Great Britain golfing stars Harry Vardon and Ted Ray returned to the United States for a lengthy tour and to compete in the 1920 U.S. Open at the Inverness Country Club in Toledo, Ohio.

Vardon's chances for a win at Inverness were considered to be in the slim-to-none category. At fifty the glory days of the six-time winner of the British Open were considered to be behind him, as evidenced by his performance in that year's British Open, when he finished fifteen strokes off the pace. It was thought he had made the trip over to the United States for the most part to keep Ray company. But to everyone's surprise, when the fourth and final round began, the fifty-year-old Vardon found himself in an unexpected place—in the lead. A one-under-par 71 in the third round had placed him atop the leaderboard by one stroke.

Vardon played the front side of the final round at even par. He parred ten and then rolled in a birdie at eleven. At this stage Vardon had a commanding five-stroke advantage, and then the calendar seemed to come into play. This United States Open was played on Thursday and Friday, with thirty-six holes being played each day. The date for the last two rounds was Friday the thirteenth.

During Vardon's play of the tenth and eleventh holes, an enormous and freakish-looking black cloud began to scale up from the horizon. To this point, the air was dead calm. As Vardon stood on the twelfth tee to tackle the longest hole at Inverness—a 522-yard uphill par five—an intense wind ignited from beneath the cloud and blasted against his face. In this brutal near gale, Vardon's drive landed way too early. His next two shots, although well struck and straight, suffered the same fate. It took a half-pitch on his fourth shot to reach the putting surface, and he two-putted for a bogey.

The cloud raced away over the horizon, but its effect on Vardon's game seemingly hung around. When Vardon arrived at the seventeenth tee, he had experienced three three-putt bogeys over the last four holes. The seventeenth at Inverness was a long par four. Vardon's drive fell in the second-rate class. It appeared the grind of a major championship was catching up to Vardon's fifty-year-old body. To reach the green now would take a superb second shot that would have to carry a ditch guarding the front of the green.

To carry his bag at Inverness, Vardon had contracted the services of forty-two-year-old Joe Horgan, the "Dean of American Caddies." In the early 1890s Horgan had begun caddying at St. Andrew's in Yonkers. Because of a price war between shipping lines, he was able to travel to Newport, Rhode Island, in 1895 for the first U.S. Amateur and the first United States Open. In the latter, Horgan carried the bag for the winner, Horace Rawlins.

Soon after Horgan returned to New York City, he changed his caddying base from St. Andrew's to the newly opened public course at Van Cortlandt Park, where, because of his duties with Rawlins at the Open, he was a celeb. Horgan's caddie stardom continued to spiral upward, as he was on the bag for Willie Anderson on three of the four occasions Anderson won the United States Open.

Horgan had caddied for Vardon during his first trip to America in 1900 and had been on his bag at the U.S. Open at Brookline in 1913.

When Vardon and Horgan reached Vardon's drive in the seventeenth fairway, Horgan advised Vardon to lay up short of the ditch and play for par by way of a chip and a one-putt. “Not now,” said old Vardon. “I'd as well be in the ditch as short.” And he went for it, with all he had. It wasn't enough. The ditch spread just four feet across. Vardon's ball came down in the middle of it. He made six. At eighteen he stopped the bleeding with a routine par. He went to the scorer's tent with a wearisome gait and signed for a six-over-par 78.

Having the leader of the third round play in the last group in the fourth round was still decades away. Harry Vardon was one of the early starters. His fellow countryman Ted Ray was several groups behind him. Ray would finish strong and take the victory. Vardon would finish in a four-way tie for second, one stroke back.

AN AMERICAN WOMAN PLAYS WITH A BRITISH ROYAL AND STIRS UP GOLF FASHION

Because of his highly regarded service in the British Army during World War I, the Prince of Wales had become a favorite of the British people. His popularity and the fact that he was the world's highest-profile eligible bachelor resulted in the press covering his almost every move. This heavy press coverage made him a top trendsetter in men's fashion.

The prince thoroughly enjoyed his fashion-plate status, which proved to be quite a challenge for his valet. When the prince traveled abroad, it took twenty-seven pieces of luggage to accommodate his extensive wardrobe.

Nowhere was the prince's impact on fashion more appreciated than on his country's golf courses. Until the prince came along, a stiff collar with a loose-fitting Norfolk-style jacket and cap were the regulation uniform for a golfer in Great Britain, unless, that is, you belonged to a club that had its own jacket, like the scarlet one worn by the members at St. Andrews. That all changed when photographs of the Prince of Wales playing in a flamboyantly colored sweater instead of a jacket appeared in newspapers across Great Britain.

In reporting the occasion, the Associated Press rightly predicted that what was worn on the course in Great Britain was about to change: "One may safely surmise that British golfers will soon give up their custom of wearing coats while playing the ancient game . . . The reason is this: The Prince of Wales has done it."

The prince's choice in golf shoes—the Kiltie, an oxford style with a tongue of fringed leather draped over the laces and eyelets—became the standard in Great Britain. The prince did not like to wear a hat on the course, but when he did, he often rotated between one for driving and fairway shots and another for putting. And for a while, he wore a beret, but golfers chose not to follow his lead on that one.

Not long after dispatching the jacket, the prince was playing in his shirtsleeves. And by the summer of 1933, he was driving a stake through the hearts of those who revered the traditions for dress on the course by showing up at the first tee in the heat of summer wearing Bermuda shorts.

That summer Bea Gottlieb, a single, twenty-something leggy blonde from New York City who played to a one handicap, was visiting Great Britain, and she "just happened" to be playing golf at one of the prince's favorite courses—Coombe Hill. After several rounds there, she caught the eye of the prince, and he dispatched his golf professional–playing companion, Archie Compston, to arrange a match for him with the young lady. They played eighteen holes and ended the day even. They played again the following day, and again the match "somehow" ended even. The next day they teed it up again, and Bea won with a score of 80 to the prince's 83. He autographed the scorecard and gave it to her, along with a box of balls; she gave him one of her irons. The news of her win over the prince got into the press and made big news in the United Kingdom and even bigger news in the United States.

The following summer, Miss Gottlieb made big news again at a ladies' amateur tournament on Long Island, doing something quite unprecedented for the time: she competed in shorts. Her choice of apparel brought a quick rebuke from the Women's Metropolitan Golf Association of New York City and stirred up quite a brouhaha all across the country. Editorials pro and con appeared in newspapers, including the *New York Times*, the *New York World-Telegram*, the *Boston Herald*, and the *Oklahoma City Oklahoman*. One Canadian city sent word it was available as a refuge, with a Montreal alderman announcing that women who wanted to play in shorts would always be welcome there.

Before the brouhaha cooled, Miss Gottlieb was pictured in her shorts in a four-column spread in the *New York American* newspaper. In the piece she fervently defended her play in shorts, stating, "Shorts were the only sensible thing," and offering up what she must have believed was the ultimate validation: "The Prince of Wales wears them."

BATTLE OF THE SEXES

The summer after he had golfed with Bea Gottlieb, the Prince of Wales had a golf match with another woman born in the United States that was far less enjoyable. She was almost twenty-five years older than Bea and very feisty. Her name was Lady Astor.

Born Nancy Witcher Langhorne in Danville, Virginia, she married a Boston blue blood when she was barely eighteen, divorced him six years later, and went to England. At twenty-seven, at the height of her striking beauty, she married the very wealthy Waldorf Astor.

Thirteen years later she became the first woman to sit in the British Parliament when she won election to the House of Commons. To say she was not greeted warmly in that formerly all-male sanctum would be an understatement. Her two chief causes, women's rights and temperance, were not favorite topics of her male counterparts, and her acid tongue made even the most skilled orators among them shy away from any verbal jousting with her—everyone except Winston Churchill. He and Lady Astor were worthy verbal adversaries. In explaining why he had shunned her when she arrived in the House of Commons, Churchill once told Astor her presence there in the previously male sanctum had made him feel "as if a woman had come into my bathroom and I had only the sponge to defend myself." Astor retorted, "You are not handsome enough to have worries of that kind."

Their most famous verbal exchange came at a banquet where the two were seated beside each other and Churchill was overindulging in strong drink. This upset Lady Astor, and she scolded him, saying, "Winston, if I were married to you, I'd put poison in your coffee." To which Churchill replied in a moderately slurred manner, "Nancy if I were married to you, I'd drink it."

Lady Astor established another first when, much to the dismay of her male counterparts, she became the first woman to compete in the Parliamentary Golf Tournament. And with a swing one newspaper described "as well deserving of the term grooved," she had delivered a severe blow to the egos of many of her male chauvinist colleagues by knocking them out of the match play tournament.

Later in the same summer he had played with Bea Gottlieb, the Prince of Wales, thanks to a royalty exemption, joined 127 participants from the House of Commons, the House of Lords, and other high-level government posts in the Parliamentary Golf Tournament.

Playing his best golf ever with a handicap of eleven, the prince found himself in the semifinals against Lady Astor, setting up one of the most interesting match-ups the long-running tournament had ever produced. To try and avoid having he and Lady Astor face the pressure of a large gallery, the time and location of their match was a closely guarded secret. This attempt at secrecy would have worked had it not been for the two participants. Word spread around London like wildfire when they both showed up at Walton-Heath, the host course, four hours before their midafternoon match to work on their games on the practice tee and green.

Lady Astor broke for lunch, but the prince stayed on the practice green, working with such a large number of balls it looked like a hailstorm had just pelted it. When his opponent returned to the course shortly before their scheduled tee time, a host of spectators appeared from nowhere and got a chance to listen to Lady Astor upbraid host professional James Braid on how far back he had moved the red tees for the match.

Lady Astor was playing at a handicap of twenty, so the prince would be giving her nine strokes, and given the number of victories his fifty-two-year-old opponent had notched over the years, she knew how to manage her game in competition and was clearly getting better with age; this would be her second appearance in the semifinals, with the first having occurred just two years earlier.

On the first hole, Lady Astor appeared to have the advantage when she put her approach shot inside of 6 feet, but she couldn't convert her birdie putt, and the prince escaped with a half. On the second hole, the prince seemed poised to grab the advantage when he reached the 425-yard par four in two, with a superb long iron approach shot. All that pre-round time on the practice green was obviously for naught, as he four-putted and allowed Lady Astor, who took four shots to reach the green, to walk away with a half.

Over the next four holes, Lady Astor had the momentum. She played steadily, while the prince continued to have severe putting problems. At the seventh hole, the prince was in a bad way. He was one down in the match, and his approach shot had run across the green and lodged itself in a bush. He had to take a penalty stroke for an unplayable lie, and then he flubbed his chip shot, and it barely trickled onto the green. But then his putter suddenly came alive, and he drained his very lengthy putt to escape with a half.

Lady Astor seemed unaffected by the prince's running in a gagger and promptly put him two down on the eighth hole. The prince came right back and took the ninth, to cut her advantage back to one. They halved ten and eleven, and the turning point of the match came at the par-three twelfth.

The prince bunkered his tee shot and then left his first attempt from the sand in the bunker. Given the circumstances, his next shot had to be rated as one of the best of his golfing career as he made a sterling recovery, blasting his ball to within a few inches of the hole for a gimme bogey. Lady Astor missed a knee knocker for par that would have given her the hole, and from that point, the match was all Wales, and he closed her out at the seventeenth hole when he went two up with one hole to play.

In the final the next week at the Coombe Hill Golf Club, the prince went up against a spirited sixty-seven-year-old House of Commons member, George Lambert, who carried a handicap just two strokes higher than his. Fortunately for the prince, the location of where the final was going to be played fared much better in the secrecy category, and only three spectators and a reporter witnessed the contest, which was a match in name only. Lambert took command early in the contest and closed out the prince when he went five up with four holes left to play.

BEN AND TERRIBLE TOMMY

In March 1957 the *Sports Illustrated* issue with the first segment of Ben Hogan's "Five Modern Fundamentals of Golf" was released. This first segment covered the grip. The remaining installments, covering stance, posture, backswing, and downswing, would follow in the next four issues. Soon thereafter, the five segments would be released in book form and become the top golf instructional book of all time.

The winter before that edition of *Sports Illustrated* hit the streets, Tommy Bolt, the PGA Tour's all-time leader in temper tantrums and club throwing, which rightly earned him the nicknames of Thunder Bolt, Tempestuous Tommy, and Terrible Tommy, made a winter trip to Fort Worth, Texas. He was having a big problem with a hook and practically got down on his knees and begged Ben Hogan to help him get rid of it.

During their sessions at Hogan's Shady Oaks Country Club in Fort Worth, Hogan adjusted Tommy's grip, moving his left hand more on top of the club. It took plenty of additional practice after he left Fort Worth. But after about a month, Bolt "no longer feared the hook."

Two years later Tommy picked up the biggest win of his career. It came in Fort Worth. It was the Colonial Invitational, an event Hogan had won four times. Tommy kept his cool for four days to win by one stroke over Ken Venturi. Hogan had a shot at denying Bolt his win at Colonial. He needed a birdie to tie him when he stepped onto the eighteenth tee in the final round. Ironically, Ben hit an atrocious hook and made a double bogey, which dropped him into a tie for fourth place.

The Colonial Invitational did not hold its place as Tommy's biggest win for long. Five weeks later he won the United States Open in his native state of Oklahoma at the Southern Hills Country Club in Tulsa.

Tommy was tied or in the lead for the first three rounds. In the final round, he shot a solid even par to win by four strokes over second-place finisher Gary Player.

Tommy, who did not go on the professional tour until he was in his early thirties, did not have the best relationship with the press. This presented itself after the second round, when Tommy took a reporter for the Tulsa paper to task because of a misprint in its morning edition. Tommy was forty years old at the time, but the paper had said he was forty-nine. The Tulsa writer apologized for the typographical error.

"Typographical error, hell," Tommy said. "It was a perfect four and a perfect nine."

HIGHLY REGARDED CBS GOLF COMMENTATOR GOES OUT OF BOUNDS

In May 1995 Valerie Helmbreck, a reporter for the *Wilmington (de) News Journal*, entered a CBS Television trailer at the Dupont Country Club on the first day of McDonald's LPGA Championship. Helmbreck had been a reporter for her paper for twelve years. She had formerly been the paper's TV critic, but her current assignment was feature writing. Helmbreck had arranged to interview a man the *New York Times* once described as a verbal colossus, Ben Wright, CBS's longtime and highly regarded golf commentator. Wright was on hand to be part of the network's coverage of the event on the weekend.

Wright was always at the top of his game when working CBS's signature golf event: the Masters. A transplant from Great Britain, he covered the fifteenth hole with a flair all his own, with comments like "A gentle zephyr at his back" or "He will leave nothing behind in his shoes. He will leap at this one." Even his criticism had class. On a missed putt by Greg Norman, he said, "You can call that a great chance squandered." But on this day Wright's "class club" may have been missing from his bag.

Helmbreck entered the trailer planning to do a piece on the differences between televising an LPGA event and a PGA tournament. She left with a far more different story, a very explosive one.

In her story, which ran the next day, Helmbreck described in detail a rant Wright went on about the sexual orientation of some of the members of the LPGA Tour and how women's breasts inhibited their golf swings. As one would expect, it created quite a firestorm. CBS called Wright back to headquarters, and he vehemently denied making the comments. Back in Wilmington, the *News Journal* and Helmbreck were just as vehement in their defense of the accuracy of the story.

Wright survived but only temporarily. Seven months later he made statements to a writer for *Sports Illustrated* about Mrs. Helmbreck's personal life that were blatantly false. A few days after that, CBS announced that Wright would no longer be a part of its golf team He was being suspended with pay for the duration of his current contract, which still had approximately three years to run, and there were no plans for his return.

SLOW PLAY RESULTS IN A U.S. SENATOR DECKING A PROMINENT DC SURGEON

The Chevy Chase Club in Chevy Chase, Maryland, was organized in 1892 to offer a club that focused on sports and recreation outside the commotion of nearby Washington DC. In June 1924 the commotion the organizers had sought to escape paid a visit to their golf course and made headlines.

On what was a pleasant June day, a foursome of United States senators were playing the twelfth hole. Two of them were on the green, and two were nearby looking for a shot to the green that had gone astray. The group behind them was a threesome. As the search for the errant shot dragged on, the threesome requested they be allowed to play through, and permission was granted.

As the threesome was teeing off on the next hole, the four senators arrived. Words were exchanged between Senator Joesph Robinson of Arkansas and the threesome's Dr. James F. Mitchell, a noted Washington DC surgeon, concerning the golf etiquette of the threesome. The exchange heated up quickly, with Robinson threatening to hit Mitchell and with Mitchell retorting: "You are going to hit me, are you. You wouldn't hit anybody!"

Mitchell was wrong. Robinson delivered a blow that sent him to the ground, which prompted the others to intervene.

There was an investigation of the incident by the Board of Governors of Chevy Chase. It resulted in Senator Robinson being temporarily suspended from the club, and later that suspension was made permanent.

WALTER'S SHENANIGANS

In 1935 Paul Gallico was still a few years away from giving up sportswriting to become a novelist. He was covering the second Masters in Augusta, Georgia, for the *New York Daily News*. The evening after the first round, he decided to take in some of Augusta's nightlife. Gallico was still taking it in at 2:00 a.m. when he bumped into a Masters participant in a gambling hall, eleven-time major champion Walter Hagen. Hagen's face was rose-colored. He had a stack of roulette chips in one hand and a tall glass of scotch in the other.

Gallico passed along his encounter with Hagen to his fellow press members during the second round. Walter had shot a 73 in the first round. In the second round, he shot a three-under-par 69. Afterward he was quizzed by the press about what time he had gone to bed. Walter stated that he had slipped into bed at six in the morning for a quick snooze, before rising around nine. He had a glass of orange juice for breakfast and headed off for his 11:00 a.m. tee time. Walter's play would slip in the final rounds, and he would finish well back in the pack.

From the early days of his career, Walter's late-night activities and late arrival to the course had been his trademarks. His habit of being notoriously late for starting times seems unthinkable given the strict rules of today. But times were different for most of his era. He once arrived on the first tee for the Pasadena Open in a tuxedo. His playing partners had already completed two holes. He was taken by car to the third tee to catch up with his playing partners. After completing the eighteenth hole, Walter was allowed to go back and play the first two holes alone.

Even if he had not been up all night, Walter would want his competitors to think he had. He would roll the clothes he was going to wear into a wad before putting them on to make it look like he had worn them all night. On other occasions he would play the first couple of holes in his dancing shoes before changing into his golf shoes.

Walter's late arrival habit finally caught up with him. In 1940, at the U.S. Open at the Canterbury Golf Club outside Cleveland, Ohio, he showed up late for his third-round tee time and was disqualified by USGA officials. It was his twenty-third appearance in the U.S. Open, and it would be the last time he took part in the event.

ARNOLD PALMER'S HEARING SPURRED HIM TO TWO OF HIS MASTERS WINS

The first occasion when Arnold Palmer's ears came into play was in the 1958 Masters. He played a practice round with Ben Hogan, and Palmer played poorly. In the locker room after the round, Palmer overheard Hogan asking another former Masters champion, Jackie Burke Jr.: "Tell me something, Jackie. How in the hell did Palmer get an invitation to the Masters?" Hearing the remark stung Arnold, and he decided he would show Hogan why he had been invited.

Arnold had the lead after the third round, and thanks to an eagle at the thirteenth hole in the final round, he was able to hold on to the lead. He earned his first of four green jackets by one stroke.

The second occasion for Arnold's ears to come into play was in the final round of the 1962 Masters. The par-three sixteenth hole at Augusta is where it can all end for a player's hopes in the final round. Losing a stroke here, this close to the finish, is often fatal. A player's fortitude and his ability to overcome adversity are often put to an extreme test here.

In 1962 Arnold found himself in just that kind of situation. He had started the day two strokes in the lead, but he was two strokes behind when he reached the sixteenth tee. A few moments later, his prospects looked even bleaker. His tee shot was long and ran off the green, leaving him with a very difficult forty-five-foot downhill chip back to the hole.

As the gallery was being moved out of the way so he could play his shot, Arnold overheard Jimmy Demaret, who was the commentator for the hole for CBS's television coverage, tell the viewing audience essentially that Arnold's goose was cooked. Arnold had been out of focus all day, but Demaret's negative comments got Arnold's competitive engine fired up and his mind tightly focused for the first time all day.

Since the green slanted toward the pin, Arnold played an ultra-soft chip. The ball landed on the green like a marshmallow and headed for the hole with just enough speed to get to the cup. It trickled up to the hole and bumped into the flagstick and then wedged itself gingerly between the stick and the cup.

"Arnie's Army," which had been in virtual retreat all day, exploded. Another patented charge by their leader was underway. While the thunderous roar was taking place, Arnold made his birdie official. He strode up to the hole and shifted the flagstick, and the ball dropped into the bottom of the cup.

Arnold would birdie seventeen and par eighteen to force an eighteen-hole playoff the following day with Dow Finsterwald and Gary Player, which he would win by three strokes over Player and nine over Finsterwald.

JOHN DALY WINS FOR THE FIRST TIME IN A "SOBER" FASHION

In early May 1994 John Daly, back on tour for just a few weeks after serving a four-month suspension for unprofessional behavior, got up and down from a bunker at the seventy-second hole to win the Bell South Classic by one stroke over Brian Henninger and defending champion Nolan Henke.

Daly's suspension was the result of his having picked up his ball and pocketed it instead of holing out late in the 1993 season during the Kapalua International on Maui. There had been several other incidents involving Daly over the season in which his behavior could best be described as erratic. PGA Tour commissioner Deane Beman had seen enough and suspended Daly from the tour for four months.

Upon his return from suspension, Daly's play was a long way from a winner's check. Three weeks before his win at the Bell South in the Greater Greensboro Open, Daly shot an opening-round 78 and then, disheartened, went back to his hotel room and shaved his head. Hairless, he played even worse in the second round, shooting 84 and missing the cut by a mile. But the next week at Houston, he turned it around and finished seventh. At Atlanta he was at the top or near the top of the leaderboard for the entire tournament.

Daly, who had spent part of his four-month suspension in an alcohol treatment facility, said the five-footer he sank for birdie at the par-five eighteenth for the win in Atlanta looked like it was twenty feet long. In his post-victory news conference, he told reporters this was the first tournament he had ever won sober. Before his stay at the alcohol treatment center, he had been reportedly drinking a bottle of Jack Daniels a day. He said he intended to celebrate this victory by eating a dozen donuts.

Being on the wagon did not last much longer for Daly, as he was soon drinking again.

IT WAS AN ODD FINISH TO A PLAYOFF

In 2001 Phil Mickelson sought his second straight win in front of his hometown fans at the Buick Invitational (now the Farmers Insurance Open) at Torrey Pines in San Diego. The year before, Phil had finished four strokes ahead of the second-place finisher, his arch-rival Tiger Woods.

This year, after seventy-two holes, Phil was atop the leaderboard, ahead of Tiger by two strokes. But he was not alone atop the leaderboard. Tied with him for first were Davis Love III and Frank Lickliter.

Phil, Love, and Lickliter returned to the eighteenth tee for a playoff. Each of the three reached the par-five eighteenth in two. Phil had a seventy-foot downhill putt that he sent seven feet past the hole. Lickliter, from thirty-five feet above the hole, was a little long, slipping two feet past the cup. Love, from just twelve feet above the hole, charged his putt and went five feet past the cup. Phil and Love made their knee knockers, and Lickliter made his short one.

The playoff then moved to the 208-yard par-three sixteenth. It had been the most difficult hole on the course that day, with only five birdies being recorded by the field. Phil and Lickliter found the green with their tee shots and two-putted for par. Love's tee shot plugged in the bunker on the right side of the green, and he could not get up and down for his par and was eliminated.

Phil and Lickliter moved to the tee box at the 425-yard par-four seventeenth hole. Phil hit a horrendous tee shot that sliced well left into the trees, leaving the door wide open for Lickliter, who was vying for his first PGA Tour victory. But he slammed it shut, hitting his tee shot into the trees with Phil's. Both balls were ultimately found, and both were out of bounds. The two then returned to the tee with a penalty shot added and hit their third shots.

Lickliter's drive was solid and in the fairway. Phil's shot was almost a carbon copy of his first drive. It was headed into the trees on the left side of the fairway. As his ball was about to go into the trees, Phil yelled, "Spit it out." As if on command, his ball ricocheted to the right off a tree limb and landed in the rough, in a position that gave him a clear line to the green.

On their approaches Phil's ended up twenty feet from the hole; Lickliter was much closer, at just twelve feet. Phil's putt came up just short, leaving him a tap-in for a double bogey. Lickliter went for the win, but his putt for bogey was too strong and raced by the hole some five feet, and his putt for double bogey slid by the left edge of the cup, giving Phil the win.

TWO AMERICAN STANDOUTS HAVE PROBLEMS IN GREAT BRITAIN

Six months after Francis Ouimet's historic win at the 1913 U.S. Open at Brookline, where he took down British golfing greats Harry Vardon and Ted Ray in an eighteen-hole playoff, a throng of local well-wishers gathered on the dock in Boston Harbor to wish him a bon voyage. Ouimet was about to depart for Great Britain to compete in the British Amateur and the British Open, with a trip to Paris sandwiched between the two to play in the French Amateur.

Ouimet had obtained a new white canvas golf bag for the trip. One person in the group of well-wishers decided that everyone should sign Ouimet's bag to give him good luck. The last person in the crowd to step forward and sign was Eddie Lowery, the now eleven-year-old, who had been Ouimet's caddie at Brookline. In a bold free hand, he inscribed just two letters: *E. L.* He then stepped back and looked yearningly at the huge ocean liner. One could tell he wanted to slip on board and stow away.

Ouimet arrived six weeks in advance of the British Amateur, to get familiar with the country and its courses, especially the host course: Royal St. George's. But despite plenty of preparation, he played poorly. He only made it to the match play event's second round before falling to an unheralded British amateur.

The following week, he traveled to Paris for the French Amateur and found France more to his liking. The French Amateur had a small field of twenty-nine, with thirteen being from the United States. Ouimet was easily the class of the field and won the title with relative ease.

When he returned to Great Britain for the British Open at Prestwick, Ouimet again played poorly. He was fifteen strokes behind the leader, Harry Vardon, at the end of two rounds. Vardon would go on to win the title, while Ouimet continued to struggle and finished twenty-three strokes off the pace.

While Ouimet's journey to Britain had been a big disappointment, another American golfer's journey across the Atlantic had been a disaster. John McDermott was the winner of the 1911 and 1912 United States Opens. He used these wins to become the first golf professional to cash in on endorsements. His financial success was short-lived as a result of bad investments.

McDermott decided at the last moment to attempt to play in the 1914 British Open. On the last leg of his trip, he missed a vital ferry connection by less than ten minutes. This delayed his arrival at Prestwick by twenty-four hours, and he missed the first round of the tournament's two-day qualifier. The tournament's officials were considering giving McDermott special consideration and getting him into the field. But McDermott nixed it, stating that it would not be fair to the other competitors.

Several days later McDermott boarded an ocean liner for his return to the United States. An hour into the voyage, the liner collided with a freighter in the English Channel. The liner suffered extensive damage below the waterline, and the passengers were ordered into lifeboats. Before the lifeboats could be lowered into the water, the crew was able to stabilize the ship, and it limped back into port.

Physically, McDermott was okay, but his behavior changed radically after the experience. The brashness and abundant self-confidence he had previously displayed were gone. He played in the 1914 United States Open in Chicago but was not a factor. Several months later he suffered a breakdown in the pro shop of the Atlantic City Country Club. For the rest of his life, he would be in and out of mental health hospitals.

TICKER TAPES AND TOOTS

A ticker tape parade is a long-standing tradition in New York City that honors the accomplishments of individuals or teams. The honorees are showered with confetti as they are driven down the Canyon of Heroes—Broadway between the Battery and City Hall—in an open vehicle. The list of honorees is a who's who of great accomplishments: Charles Lindbergh, Winston Churchill, Generals MacArthur and Eisenhower, polar explorer Richard Byrd, and U.S. astronauts.

In 1926 Bobby Jones became the first individual from the world of sports to be so honored for winning that year's British Open. He was honored again in his grand slam year of 1930, after his return from Great Britain, where he had won the British Open and the British Amateur.

In 1953 Ben Hogan, who had already won that year's Masters and the U.S. Open, was honored when he returned from winning the British Open. Immediately after the conclusion of the parade, Hogan made a beeline to the nation's premier watering hole at 51 West Fifty-First Street: Toots Schor's Restaurant.

Toots was a former underwear salesman and bouncer. He was a burly guy, high-spirited, and a huge sports fan. And he possessed superstar talent when it came to making friends. Toots had opened his establishment in 1940. Joe DiMaggio soon became a regular, and other big names in sports, entertainment, and other high-profile walks of life followed him through its doors, making it one of the top spots to be in New York City for over two decades.

While its name included the word *restaurant*, Toots called his place a saloon. During its run it earned the tag of best sports bar ever. While it lacked the decor of today's typical sports bar—no memorabilia and no televisions—it was in a world of its own when it came to who was there. Besides the likes of DiMaggio, Jack Dempsey, Frank Gifford, and Mickey Mantle, you could witness Yogi Berra rubbing elbows with Ernest Hemingway or a Supreme Court justice enjoying a drink just a few feet away from a mafia kingpin.

The winners of the Masters from 1953 through 1960 were expected to stay in Augusta for a few extra days to play a round of golf with one of Augusta National's members: Dwight Eisenhower, the president of the United States. This round with the president of the United States presented a problem for 1955 Masters champion Cary Middlecoff. Cary wanted to get to one of his special places as soon as possible to celebrate his victory, and this locale was nowhere near Augusta National. Toots Schor's Restaurant was 775 miles away.

To handle his quandary between Toots Schor's and a round of golf with the president, Cary Middlecoff opted to do what Billy Joe Patton had done the previous year. Patton, an amateur, had stood the golf world on its ear in 1954 by almost winning the Masters. He ultimately finished one stroke out of a playoff for the Masters crown with Ben Hogan and Sam Snead that Snead had won.

Before the 1954 tournament was even over, President Eisenhower sent word from Washington that not only did he want to play a round with the winner. He also wanted to play eighteen with Billy Joe Patton. This posed a problem for Patton. Being an amateur, he had a job as a lumber salesman that he needed to tend to back in his hometown of Morganton, North Carolina. Patton decided he would do a little driving. He climbed in his car the next day and drove the 220 miles back to Morganton, checked on how things were at the office, and then drove back to Augusta for his round with the president.

Middlecoff decided he would fly to New York City, go to Toots Schor's, and celebrate, and then fly back to Augusta. The Masters champion was more than well received when he walked through the doors at Toots's, and quite a celebration ensued. The next day he flew back to Augusta to tee it up with the president of the United States.

A SPECIAL FRIENDSHIP

In May 1964, at age seventy-three, former President Dwight Eisenhower played for the first time in front of a paying gallery. The occasion was a fundraiser for the Pennsylvania Heart Association. The locale was the famed Merion Golf Club in Ardmore, Pennsylvania, the site of numerous major golf championships. Ike's playing partner was Arnold Palmer. He and Arnie had first met in 1958, and the two soon developed a powerful friendship. Their opponents at Merion were three-time Masters champion Jimmy Demaret and actor Ray Bolger, who had played the Scarecrow in *The Wizard of Oz*. The two teams squared off in a match play alternating-shot format before a crowd of approximately six hundred people.

Ike and Arnie took the match, and after it was all over, Arnie addressed the crowd, telling them his partner had carried him all day—and that was no exaggeration. By seventy-three-year-old standards, Ike had given a superb performance. He had looked a little rough on the practice tee, and before heading for the first tee, he had had to gulp down some aspirin for his bursitis.

But once the match was on, the competitive spirit that had been his trademark throughout his life kicked in. He split the fairway with a

220-yard drive on the first hole. Arnie played the next shot to within 10 feet of the pin, and then the crowd roared when Ike drained the putt for an opening birdie and a quick one-up lead. On the eighth hole Arnie's errant tee shot ended up in the rough and put the team in a bit of a tight spot. But Ike came through in the clutch, hitting a short iron from a hanging lie, over water and a bunker. The shot came to rest 3 feet from the pin to set up another birdie, which gave him and Arnie a three-up lead. Demaret and Bolger rallied, and after the tenth hole, they had cut the lead to just one.

On the way to the eleventh green, Ike paused to study a plaque that read, "On Sept. 27, 1930, on this hole, Robert Tyre Jones, Jr. completed his grand slam by winning the U.S. Amateur Championship." Reading about the heroics of his great friend must have inspired him. Ike set up successful birdie putts by Arnie with his approach shots at thirteen and fifteen, which once again put them three up. When the two teams halved the sixteenth hole, the match was officially over, as Demaret and Bolger were three holes down with only two holes left to play.

Ike's aide General Robert Schultz asked him if he was ready to call it a day. The president's reply was "To heck with it; let's finish it." Ike then treated the gallery to two more splendid shots. On the seventeenth he snaked in a forty-five-foot putt for birdie, and on eighteen he set up a birdie attempt for Arnie with another fine approach shot.

Ike's play had to have surprised Arnie that day, and Ike gave Arnie another big surprise two years later. Arnie's wife, Winnie, asked Mamie and Ike to come to the Palmer home in Latrobe, Pennsylvania, for a weekend as a surprise birthday present for her husband. When Arnie answered an unexpected knock on the door, he was floored. There stood Ike, who said, "Happy Birthday, Pro." Arnie later described that weekend as one of the most special of his life. Mamie and Winnie went shopping, while Arnie and Ike hung out in Arnie's den watching football games and swapping stories.

SPOUSES, EX-SPOUSES, AND SIGNIFICANT OTHERS

In the 1988 Masters final round, Sandy Lyle displayed a little fancy footwork with a Scottish jig after draining a ten-foot putt on the eighteenth green to win by one stroke. Lyle credited his girlfriend, a physiotherapist, with helping him get through the tournament. He was battling a head cold throughout the four rounds, and she would tickle his toes at night. Lyle said this made him laugh and cleared his head.

A few days after his victory at the PGA Championship in 1933, at the Blue Mound Country Club outside Milwaukee, Gene Sarazen told a Chicago reporter that it had been a letter from his wife, Mary, that he received just before the tournament began that had spurred him to victory. Although Mary was present in spirit, she was where Gene believed a wife needed to be when her husband was competing in a major championship—at home. Over the years Gene had developed this attitude, believing that having one's spouse at a big event was too much of a distraction. After his win at Milwaukee, Gene espoused his views on the matter in a magazine interview:

The hand that rocks the cradle is rocking a lot of golf's finest professionals into bankruptcy and mediocrity . . . The saddest thing in golf isn't a muffed two-foot putt that loses a big championship, it's those zealous, jealous, gossiping wives of our playing professionals who haunt their husbands and watch them fire every shot in a money tournament or open championship. It's time the shackled pros arose in a body and told them to stay home . . . [and] sew buttons on the old man's shirts . . . Those women are the curse of golf today.

President Warren Harding's inauguration took place on March 4, 1921. Just a few days later, his golf playing created a firestorm of negative press because, on his first Sunday in the White House, he chose to skip church and head to the golf course. The first lady, Florence Harding, who the newly sworn-in president called "the boss," took point in handling the firestorm. She addressed the press and firmly declared that she could assure them it would not happen again.

Babe Didrickson met her husband, George Zaharias, a three hundred–pound pro wrestler, when organizers of a 1937 pro-am tournament, as a gag, paired Babe, George, and a minister together for the event. Babe and George married a year later.

George was always in the gallery near Babe during a tournament. His trademark was that he always seemed to have a cigar in his mouth. This was an asset for Babe. When she needed assistance with wind direction, she would look over to George, who then would exhale a couple of hearty puffs from his cigar.

Lee Trevino was having doubts on the eve of the final round of the 1984 PGA Championship at Shoal Creek Golf and Country Club in Birmingham, Alabama. Lee was questioning whether at age forty-four he still had it in him to hold onto his one-stroke lead in the final round. His wife, Claudia, gave him the thought he needed. She told him, "Your clubs do not know how old you are." Lee shot a 69 in the final round and won by three strokes.

It was an all-American final in the 1951 British Amateur at Royal Porthcawl Golf Club in Wales between Dick Chapman and Charles Coe. Chapman, age forty, lived in the heart of Pinehurst, North Carolina. He was the son of a very successful father. This allowed him to work part-time as a bond salesman and devote the rest of his time to golf.

Chapman had won the U.S. Amateur at Winged Foot in 1940 and had finished second in the British Amateur in 1947 and 1950. In the 1951 thirty-six-hole final against Coe, Chapman led two up after eighteen holes. But at the twenty-fourth hole, he made a double bogey, and he lost it. He hurled his cigarette to the ground, angrily kicked the turf, and bawled out his caddie. After the fit of temper, his wife took him aside and let Chapman have it. "What are you," she demanded, "a man or a mouse?"

Chapman was all man from that point forward. He unleashed a brilliant blazing finish with a burst of three birdies over the next five holes and missing a hole in one by inches to swamp Coe and take the title by a count of five up with four to play.

In the final of the 1930 PGA Championship at the Fresh Meadow Country Club in Queens, New York, Tommy Armour and Gene Sarazen battled it out for thirty-six holes, with Armour taking a one-up victory. Tommy and Gene had become close friends over the years. As they posed on the first tee that day for photographers, their well-earned reputation as golf fashion plates was on full display.

In 1922 Tommy's wife, Consuelo, had put Gene on the road to high fashion. Shortly after Gene's first win on the PGA Tour at the Southern Open in 1922 in New Orleans, Consuelo had pulled him aside to talk about his attire. She was very blunt. Consuelo told him he dressed like a caddie instead of a golfer. She then gave him the contact information for the gentleman who supplied Tommy with his golfing apparel.

Consuelo wasn't at Fresh Meadow to witness Tommy and Gene battle it out in 1930. She and Tommy had gone through a messy divorce. She had made headlines a few months earlier when she filed suit seeking $670,000 (roughly $13 million today) from Tommy. She eventually ended up settling for a lesser amount.

In 1967 Tom Nieporte became the last club professional to win a PGA Tour event. He did so in dramatic fashion, birdieing the final hole at the Bob Hope Desert Classic to win by one stroke over Doug Sanders.

Nieporte, the pro at the Piping Rock Club on Long Island, had traveled to California with several club members to play in the Bing Crosby Pro-Am at Pebble Beach. He played poorly in the event, winning only eighty-four dollars. He called his wife, who was eight months pregnant with their eighth child, to tell her he was on the way home. She urged him to stay and play in the LA Open in hopes he would play better and recoup some of the expenses of the trip.

It turned out to be a wise move. Nieporte played much better, finishing fourteenth, and picked up a nice check by the standards of the day. With an airline ticket in his pocket, he again called his wife, who was now twenty days from her delivery date, to tell her he was on the way home. Since his play had dramatically improved and based on his LA Open finish he would not have to qualify, she urged him to stay out one more week and play in the Hope, and he did.

After the first round, the decision looked suspect, as Tom posted a four-over 76. But he caught fire from there, posting three straight rounds of 68 and a closing round of 69 to win the ninety-hole event's $17,600 first prize. Child number eight came a few weeks later. In two years a ninth child would arrive.

Lynn Burnsdale of Chicago was visiting the Davenport, Iowa, area. One day she stopped by the pro shop of the municipal course with a club that needed repair. The course's pro took care of it. Lynn liked his work, and she liked him. They were married six weeks later.

Six years later that pro, Jack Fleck, defeated Ben Hogan in a playoff to win the 1955 United States Open at the Olympic Club in San Francisco. Lynn was not standing by the eighteenth green at the finish. She was standing behind the counter at the pro shop back in Iowa, filling in for her husband while he was taking down Ben Hogan.

At the first hole in the second round of the 1979 Masters, Mac McLendon's approach shot missed the green, and it flew into the gallery and struck a woman in the head. The dazed woman was taken to the first aid station and then to the hospital for X-rays. After the woman checked out all right at the hospital, she returned to the course and started following Mac McLendon again. It wasn't because she now felt she had a special bond with him. She already had that, for she was Mrs. Mac McLendon.